A Sense of Place

A collection of new Scottish writing

WAVERLEY
BOOKS

edinburgh
(edɪnbʌrə) *n.*
UNESCO City of
Literature

 Scottish
Arts Council

SCOTTISH **PUBLISHERS** ASSOCIATION

Published 2005 by Waverley Books Ltd, New Lanark, Scotland,
in association with the Scottish Publishers Association and
Edinburgh UNESCO City of Literature

A catalogue record for this book is available from the British Library

ISBN 10: 1 902407 34 2
ISBN 13: 978 1 902407 34 0

Printed and bound in Poland

POLSKABOOK

A Sense of Place

Acknowledgements

A Sense of Place began as a writing competition. This idea was conceived to draw attention to the importance of new writing in Scotland, about Scotland and to promote both the Scottish Publishers Association (www.scottishbooks.org) and Edinburgh UNESCO City of Literature (www.cityofliterature.com). The UNESCO status was designated on the city to celebrate Scotland's literary heritage.

The competition was run in conjuction with Waverley Books and was open to short narrative non-fiction pieces of 800–3,500 words, inspired by the theme of 'Scotland' and the title of this book, *A Sense of Place.*

Four judges selected 25 essays from the 200 submitted. The judges were Alison Bowden, Rights Manager for Edinburgh University Press; Sophy Dale, Development Manager for Edinburgh UNESCO City of Literature; Mike Miller, Publisher of Waverley Books, and Lorraine Fannin, Director of the Scottish Publishers Association.

Entries were received on a wide variety of topics and from as far afield as Australia and America. Overall, the judges were looking for pieces of writing that strongly evoked a sense of location. They commend and thank all those who entered the competition and in particular the 25 writers whose work is included in this collection.

The publishers gratefully acknowledge the following sources for permission to use copyright material:

the extracts from 'Climbing Suilven', 'By Achmelvich Bridge', 'Sheep Dipping, Achmelvich', 'Humanism' and 'A Man in Assynt' by Norman MacCaig are published by permission of Polygon, an imprint of Birlinn Ltd

the extracts from *Trainspotting* (originally published by Secker & Warburg) and *Porno* (originally published by Jonathan Cape) by Irvine Welsh, both available in paperback published by Vintage. Reprinted by permission of The Random House Group Ltd.

the extracts from *Collected Poems and Songs* (pp 29, 84, 94, 142 and 143) by Hamish Henderson (ed) Raymond Ross are published by permission of the estate of Hamish Henderson and Curly Snake Press

the extract from *Elegies for the Dead in Cyrenaica* (p 18) by Hamish Henderson (originally published by EUSPB), and 'It was in You That it A' Began' by Hamish Henderson in *The People's Past: Scottish Folk, Scottish History* (ed) Edward J. Cowan (originally published by EUSPB), are published by permission of the estate of Hamish Henderson and Polygon, an imprint of Birlinn Ltd.

the extract from Lorca's 'El poeta in Nueva York' translated by Paul Pinding on p 131 of his *Lorca: The Gay Imagination* is published by permission of Gay Men's Press

the extract from 'Ithaca' by Cavafy translated by Robert Liddell on p 154 of his *Cavafy: A Biography* (originally published by Gerald Duckworth & Co), published by permission of the Duckworth Media Group and Robert Liddell as translator

the extract from *The Axion Esti* (p 31) by Odysseus Elytis translated by Edmund Keeley and George Savidis, published by permission of Anvil Press Poetry and Edmund Keeley and George Savidis as translators

Contents

Foreword

Tom Devine

This fine collection of evocative essays and stories ranges widely across Scotland from Assynt in the far North to the Solway Firth in the Border country, from the cities of Edinburgh, Glasgow and Dundee to the small villages and farms of Scotland's rural regions. The writing is diverse, sometimes lyrical, often factual and perceptive, occasionally humorous. What comes through is a veritable kaleidoscope of views on 'a sense of place' in Scotland at the beginning of the new millennium.

For a historian like myself, the collection makes fascinating reading because many of the chapters capture in vivid prose a nation experiencing a rate of economic, social and cultural change which has been unprecedented in Scottish history for many generations. Indeed, I would argue that not since the era of the Industrial Revolution has Scotland gone through such a process of transformation. The society of the 1950s was not unlike that of a century before but since the 1970s and 1980s that old world has passed into history with de-industrialisation, increasing affluence, changes in social structure, the revolution in the position of women and much else.

These trends come through strongly in several of the essays as many of the authors have lived through these profound changes.

Thus, several contain both detailed description of, and some nostalgia for, the old days which are now but memories. Such themes as the movement of people from rural areas as mechanisation on the farms became dominant, the disappearance of heavy industry in the wake of international competition, and the vibrant cultures associated with the world we have lost are all brought vividly to life at a deeply personal level.

The authors note, however, that there is much to be welcomed in a nation which is breaking free from stasis, greyness and inertia. For instance, Dundee, the old jute capital, is being transformed, according to Andrew Murray Scott, with 40 per cent of male workers in the city having middle-class jobs and nearly 28,000 students attending the universities and colleges – 'the nightlife is literally jumping.' For Michael Turnbull, Edinburgh in the 1950s resembled 'Soviet Russia'. Princes Street was 'full of little old ladies tightly wrapped in dark-brown coats.'

As Tim Bell also shows, the once thriving port of Leith was in decline for much of the 20th century; matters were made worse by the decanting of the people in housing schemes to the west of Leith at Pilton, Pennywell, Muirhouse. The authorities thought they were acting in everyone's best interest by clearing the slums but, as Bell argues eloquently:

People had left a town with its centuries-old structures, institutions and middle class, for these places that were supposed to answer the needs of a single socioeconomic group. The open spaces quickly became unattractive with broken glass and dog shit. The planners had no intention of letting shops and pubs start a business where the demand was – that sort of thing was grouped around shopping centres ... Thus is a spontaneous and healthy economic life and social intercourse stifled and stilted. Inevitably a generation grew up with little knowledge of, or stake in, wider society.

What happened to Leith was replicated in all Scotland's major cities in the 1950s. The social and cultural scars of these housing strategies remain but, with the movement to Victoria Quay of the Scottish Executive, the building of Ocean Terminal and the proliferation of new restaurants and pubs, Leith was resurgent in the 1990s. Again, the pattern of renewal was typical of urban Scotland in that decade.

The authors in this collection are therefore generally upbeat about their 'sense of place' in the Scotland of 2005. Even in the rural areas, despite the continuing crisis in farming, there are hopes for a better future, as Brian McCabe suggests when he ponders the Assynt crofters buyout of land in the Highlands.

Equally, however, several of the essayists accept that modernity has come at a cost. James Carson's Glasgow Green may have had a makeover but the east end of the city where it lies is an area of high crime, poor health, drug abuse and low incomes. The chronic inequalities in society not only linger on but may have become more visible amid growing general affluence. 'A sense of place' and its meaning therefore depends in the final analysis on where you happen to be in this social spectrum. As Paul Johnston indicates it should also include 'the needle-parks where young people waste away, the reeking pubs full of addled hard men and the fast-food "restaurants" where our children gorge themselves on poisoned pap.'

This, then, is no sociological tract written in arcane academic language but a set of vivid and personal insights into 'a sense of place' in modern Scotland by a group of new and talented authors. I recommend it most highly.

Powfoot Shore

Vivien Jones

I am often asked 'What's it like where you live?' and I'm per-
plexed every time about how to answer. What sense in describ-
ing a place when it changes with every wind and tide? Each
wind that blows up the Solway estuary sculpts the waves into
different rhythms from white-capped true sea rollers that play
piggyback with each other racing to shore to creased silk ripples that only ruffle the surface and tickle the shore. Each tide
moves sand and silt, each season's tides design a new beach,
sometimes conspiring with the moon to make a morning surprise – a smooth expanse of sand where yesterday were only
pebbles – a gelatinous line of washed-up jellyfish – and when
the wind joins in, a tide line of foam meringues that turn from
sea creatures to creatures of the air, flying along the beach.

You understand, this is not wholly a beautiful place. A
demolished factory, smashed to huge peanut-brittle slabs of
brick, wire and concrete protect the north bank behind the
beach – industrial-scale plumbing parts exposed to the public's
discomfited gaze, white, red and black bricks, some with mysterious numbers legible, in lumps and singly scattered like con-
fetti across the expanse of pebbles and sand. Flotsam (things
that have floated ashore) and jetsam (things discarded at sea)

lie among the bricks along with sea bird remains and the occasional sheep carcase. There is also the wreckage of picnickers, a kaleidoscope of plastic bags and bottles, single, always single, trainers, broken buckets and beer cans. Everything bleached pale by salt water and wind, animal skeletons turned to wind chimes.

But nature is no weakling. Among the broken building slabs the gorse spears through, filling the air with the scent of coconuts, filling the eyes with spike-yellow flowers full of intoxicated bees. Brambles, just as spiky, restrain their purple explosion until autumn, and the gentler broom fills in spaces tangled up with fireweed and convolvulus. In the heather peat bank, bog oaks, two thousand years old, poke innocuous black limbs into the air. Small, scuttling seaside rabbits have perforated the bank with runs and burrows, staying out of the way of spiralling buzzards and a pair of hen harriers that lie on the wind above the bank. Sand martins have braved the eroding sandbank to make their colony under the matted eaves of grasses curled over into space where the sand beneath has blown away. Their stringy roots hang loose, tracing fine arcs in the sand which the martins avoid with a flick of the tail.

Down the Pow river, the turquoise dart of a kingfisher on a surprise visit to the estuary startles a fishing heron, before zipping back into fresh water. Keeping 50 metres between them and any walkers on the beach, a flock of oyster-catchers turn white bellies to the sun, then black backs as they move away in a curve along the water's edge in oscillating visibility. The shore waters are an ornithologist's Lucky Bag – swans, shags, ducks, and a lone heron may be there, unpredictable delights.

Low tide uncovers virgin land as the sea abandons miles of wet sand and mud to the sun's attentions. The river course carves deeply into the mud banks, changing its channel every few years. At very low tide when the water's edge seems close to Cumbria, walkers may find the sand moulds where flounders lay, perfectly replicated among soft-scoop worm casts. Dogs and horses, liberated from leads, race joyfully over this untouched expanse and children are in very heaven. Generations of villagers have composted their garden waste here so that stubborn survivors, spikes of lemon lupins, sinuous ropes of hops and even an apple tree, flourish among the native flora. Between the road and the mean tide line, elevated tufts of dense grass called dubs, speckled with sea pinks, tolerate the salty high tides and provide a maze of escape routes for small creatures. One of the small creatures is the rare Natterjack toad which fills spring evenings with its territorial call, en masse, a raucous choir that carries across the salt marsh right into the village.

But the sun doesn't always shine. Powfoot shore in wild weather is smashed by grey, white breakers that toss whole tree trunks, stolen from other estuaries, onto the beach. The dubs are submerged and the river struggles to hold off the thrashing sea. The shoreside trees are stubby and shaved by prevailing winds to alarming bents and the long white grass lies flat to the ground. Rain drives up the Solway in opaque horizontal sheets, Cumbria disappears. After storms, the morning shore is laden with new wreckage, smashed sea birds tangled in orange and turquoise rope or nets, tree limbs trailing seaweed whilst the calmed waters, relieved of the storm's violence, suck loudly but now harmlessly on the shingle edge.

Truly, Powfoot shore is a midnight place, the stuff of fairytales, clear air humming under the infinity of space. With a Prussian blue sky, a huge full moon and a rising tide, the black head of Skiddaw is every magic mountain in folklore, rearing above a silvered Solway. Even the satellite tracking station across the estuary with its weave of antennae lit by red lights becomes mysterious and beautiful. With no moon, the dense spiral of the Milky Way curves across a sky speckled with planets, stars, satellites and aircraft, each in their own motion and, once or twice a year, the northern sky waves soft green and red beams in ripples and shafts in the free light show that is the *Aurora Borealis*.

What might one discover on a visit to this unspectacular place? A microclimate that defies all forecast perhaps. On the days when there is a band of grey cloud over Dumfries and another cloaking the Lake District hills, there is often a space of sky as blue as a sailor's eyes over the Powfoot shore, which lasts all day, allowing picnics in November and paddling in January. Powfoot shore, a modest gem on the Scottish coast.

A Postcard From Dundee

Andrew Murray Scott

Wish you were here? Dundee High Street, with Desperate Dan, Minnie and Dawg, larger than life and looking healthy and bronzed. These statues of the *Dandy* and *Beano*'s favourite characters have been popular since they appeared in the High Street in 2002. The neds did some damage at first, interfering with Minnie, but now leave them alone. Perhaps the proliferation of CCTV cameras had something to do with that. Dundee City Square is on the Internet, courtesy of a webcam, so the polis can check from the comfort of HQ that Minnie is not being tampered with on those cold winter nights and expatriate Dundonians are able to see what the weather is like back home whenever they're in danger of having an attack of euphoria. Or they could study passers-by in real time in the hope of seeing auld Erchie, the boy wha yased ti bide in Fleuchar Street ... (In Dundee, any person of male gender is 'the boy'. As in, 'the boy eh jist seen. Him ower there – boy wi thi zimmer frame!') Ah, the delights of the Dundonian leid, closest thing to the sound of a craw talking to its mate. All echs and ehs, croaky blue, a sair-throated, fully gutteral vernacular.

Dundee does not actually have many statues to show for its 1,000 years of history. The greeny-bronze dragon, like the dialect, has disappeared from the Murraygate. It's much missed by kids who used to climb over it and by the rest of the population who used to wonder at the size of the Corn Flake packet it must have come out of. There is the squat and warty statue erected in 1997 to commemorate Admiral Duncan. It's less than five feet high yet Duncan, 'Scotland's Nelson', the victor of the Battle of Camperdown, is described in the chronicles as 'tall and intrepid, a majestic character'. The statue has been described by one local as making Duncan look 'like a cross between Captain Pugwash and Toad of Toad Hall!' And Dundee's only tribute to our national hero, William Wallace – one line on a plaque commemorating three historical events, one name among three – is half-hidden behind Duncan's plinth and was, for many years, entirely obscured behind a bus drivers' wooden shelter. A hundred yards away, an obscure bronze plaque on the frontage of Pizza Hut is all that remains of the mighty Wedderburn brothers who put Dundee at the centre of Europe in the Reformation. Historical fame doesn't cut much ice in Dundee. Burns' Dundee rival, poet Robert Nicoll, who died aged 23, is entirely forgotten: his plaque in Castle Street is long gone – who knows where?

The city archivists have a storeroom of plaques that used to be displayed in the city. Where is the freestanding plaque commemorating the birthplace of a Dundonian called William Lyon Mackenzie? It was removed in 1998 and was to be re-sited after the Overgate modernisation. Mackenzie? Never heard of him! What did he do? He founded Canada. Other plaques have been 'removed for cleaning' and haven't been seen for decades. Must have been very dirty indeed! McGonagall is not forgotten. We just can't forget him, although of course he was, technically, an Edinburgh man. There is a walkway to his memory beside that 'beautiful bridge of the silv'ry Tay' so that people can walk all over his best/worst work, some of which is, incidentally, misspelled – strictly in the cause of historical accuracy, according to the red-faced authorities when this was first brought to attention. Kings, queens, writers, poets, great historical figures visited, resided and have been totally overlooked here, forgotten more absolutely than in any other town or city.

It was John Grierson who asked how you would do a portrait of a town. He wondered whether it was possible to describe a place as a single character or painting. Writers have tried to pin the unique character of Scotland's most neglected city. McGonagall of course: 'Oh, Bonnie Dundee! I must conclude my muse / And to write in praise of thee, my pen does not refuse.' Which is maybe why he has the walkway; services rendered. Dr Johnson described the place, in a 1773 'postcard' to Mrs Thrale, as 'a dirty despicable town', a bit rich given posterity noted his habit of bathing once a year whether he needed it or not! MacDiarmid derided it as 'a great industrial cul-de-sac' which is a pretty dreadful mixed metaphor even for the grand curmudgeon, and there were harsher criticisms. Of course, these were comments about a very different Dundee. Dundee now is post-industrial, much more varied in the employment opportunities it offers. The city is changing, its population from its heyday as jute capital of the world is in decline although mostly this is due to Dundonians moving over the tightly drawn city boundary into neighbouring Angus and Perth & Kinross. New people are moving into the city to replace – and refresh – the city's spirits. The most recent survey shows that 40 per cent of male workers in Dundee have middle-class jobs and nearly 28,000 students live in the city so that the nightlife is literally jumping. The city was recently judged to be the most cost-effective city for students in the UK. The horror-story schemes of the last decade are all now at the centre of regenerated hubs – Whitfield to the north is a private housing hot spot creeping out into green fields, Stobswell, Charleston, Kirkton, Ardler, St Mary's, Fintry, Hilltown – all rebuilding, thriving. Lots of government cash is going in and the dire statistics of poverty, unplanned teenage pregnancy and educational disadvantage are slowly being improved. Dundee is of course no longer a monoculture, is no longer viewed in monochrome. The Asian community is a thriving one which has embraced and been embraced by Dundonians and has given much to community life. There is a significant Chinese community, and there are many descendants of the Poles, Ukranians and Italians who settled here after the war.

In point of fact, the city is always in the process of making itself over, each new convulsion resulting in some cultural loss or other, like a baby throwing its toys out of the bath. Few of the best buildings of earlier centuries remain, although the worst – the carbuncles – often prove immovable. The council's recent attempts to demolish some of the old multistorey towers in Menzieshill in the west of the city have faced an unexpected obstacle. The SSP have set up a 'Keep our multis' campaign. Only in Dundee, the city that sent Ford with its £40m investment and 450 jobs packing to Portugal in 1988, would this kind of backwardism and Uriah Heapish proletarianism occur. Better news, however, about 'Fawlty Towers' – Tayside House, the ghastly 17-storey block that has faced the visitor at the Dundee end of the road bridge since 1976, will be demolished in 2009. Not soon enough according to most. The spaghetti of covered walkways that connected pedestrians, the railway station, the city centre and the riverfront is already being dismantled. Hooray! There are still a few great buildings surviving in Dundee: Dudhope, Mains and Claypotts Castles, the Romanesque St Mary's Forebank, the Steeple (the highest surviving medieval church tower in Scotland), Coldside Library, the old Barrack Street museum (presently disused), the McManus Galleries, and (actually) too many others to list here.

There are many fabulous niches and peaceful corners in the city. Linger awhile in the Geddes Quadrangle in the heart of Dundee University, or sit in the ancient 15th-century Howff Cemetery two minutes from City Square, or take in the view of the railway bridge from almost anywhere in the west end, or observe the modern road bridge from almost anywhere on the Hilltown. The Botanical Gardens on Riverside are a delight, Camperdown Park is a great example of an open space (although under dire threat of being 'themed') and Broughty Ferry is a wonderful place to saunter through on a sunny Saturday. You can stroll around to the Castle and further along the dunes towards Monifieth with an ice-cream cone from Visocchi's in Gray Street.

Dundee has a beauty and ambience which its artists have long sought to capture: perhaps most famously in recent times, James McIntosh Patrick's wonderful views of the west of the city. Joseph MacKenzie's realist photographs of the 1970s, the 'Trojan Ruins' of Hawkhill and Polepark, showed how complete the transformation since the war has been. Johnny Johnstone has done some wonderfully busy images of city life in the 1960s and 1970s, as if Brueghel the Elder had suddenly decided to switch to satirical cartoons. John Stoa, a commercially popular Menzieshill-based artist, has painted many fine urban scenes. Eddie Lange paints local scenes and characters as well as running a painting school in Andalucía six months of the year. The artists seem to share a common perception of Dundee as a busy city, a place of characters and hurly-burly, rather than a place of contemplative isolation. It always has been. As a former capital city, the seat of royalty, for a time the home of the Scottish mint, the centre of that intellectual ferment known as the Reformation, and as an industrial and financial behemoth, it has always been the people in the place rather than the place itself making history, characterful, even if the characters don't get much kudos in 21st-century Dundee.

But let's be fair. Modern Dundee has many good points. In Dundee you are never more than ten minutes by car from the beach or the hills and open spaces. Dundee is undoubtedly the sunniest city in Scotland – unless weather forecasters are inveterate liars. There are no midgies in Dundee. You can often see seals and dolphins in the estuary. You can bump into your friends almost every day. When I first moved to London, I'd say 'see you later' and of course never would. Yet it's not too small that it never changes. There's always something new. It coruscates. It retains possibility.

Cultural life though is impossible to predict. Poetry festivals, literary magazines and cultural events have often struggled and given up the ghost, with the obvious exceptions of the Guitar Festival and the Jazz & Blues Festival. Like Greek drama, Dundee's cultural story will (I predict) be structured in three parts:

Dundee's Cultural Story – A Tragedy

Act 1: The Denial

Denial of existence of, or any possibility whatsoever of, or any history of, cultural life in the city. McGonagall cited as proof of this (anti-cultural figure).

Act 2: The Rejections

Formation of writers' groups, some literary activity, but none to a standard sufficient for literary approval by publishers and arts bodies (all outwith the city). A literary guidebook is published which sells only in Dundee. McGonagall (the only Dundee writer the outside world has heard of) is cited as proof of the poor standard to be expected from Dundee writers.

Act 3: The Supplanting

The lack of literary activity is noticed from afar; the city is flagged as a suitable prospect for funding opportunities. Cultural parachutists descend to take up opportunities, particularly at Dundee Contemporary Arts. Much-heralded emergence of 'real' Dundee culture, purified of any taint of yir actual Dundonian experience. Nae schemies to be invited to the premiere of McGonagall The Movie (starring Richard E. Grant).

The above sour note was drafted after overhearing a conversation in the DCA between two arts apparatchiks not long after the official opening in 1999. 'How pleasant to be in Dundee,' said one. 'Yes, at long last to have a place here one is able to come to,' replied the other. I kid you not! Luckily I fought the urge to remove and eat their livers – which would only have confirmed their prejudices about Dundonians.

Who are the 'Dundee writers'? Most, like A.L. Kennedy, James Meek, W.N. Herbert and Don Paterson, have had to leave to show they were serious about their literary ambitions. But do writers 'represent' a locality? Is there something unique about a city's heritage that can only be expressed by those aware of it? Can Dundee's heritage and cultural idiom be expressed by writers who know nothing of it? Does it matter who writes it? Should writing be locally specific even at the expense of a wider readership? My belief is that there is something specific in a place's experience, its patterns of shared observation, its feelings, hopes, expectations – something to do with living at this or that precise geographical location – which is particular and precious and specific. Writers express only themselves but the consciousness which they put into words is inextricably rooted in where they live and has particular resonance for those who live in the same place. It is one person's experience of living there but is an exemplar for all others who live there. In the global marketplace, writers still carry something of the mantle of the seer, the bard, the oral tale-teller. Writing needs this kind of localisation and this resonance to and with a particular group of people, if it is to have any specific meaning. And if it does that accurately it will strike a chord with readers everywhere. You have to people a place to make it real and portray a place on the page or in art to make it exist in a shared consciousness.

Dundee tries hard to tell others about its experiences. But so far only allows these to be expressed in PR-speak not by the stories or poems of its writers and poets who remain almost invisible in the 'City of Discovery'. The PR project nevertheless wins awards for the cleverness of their slogan, which in subtext is: 'Come to Dundee and see our old boat.'

I know what you're thinking. The postcard I'm writing this on must be some size or my skill with a pen quite miraculous. Well, sorry, I'm an enthusiast for the place and just can't stop writing and talking about it. I have in fact lived in the city for 40 of my 50 years – a fact which often surprises me, although I recall my pleasure – and relief – at returning after five years in

London. How friendly the place seemed and how bright and clean! People speak to each other; the crime rate is relatively low.

Two years ago I chaired a debate at Dundee University on the theme 'Is Dundee a better place now than it was 50 years ago?' The sides were evenly matched: architectural guru Professor Charles McKean and nature writer and columnist Jim Crumley thought modern Dundee was worse, but local radio personality Ally Bally, and Henny King, the cowboy hat-wearing former director of the Dundee Octocentenary Celebrations, disagreed. The 300 folks in the audience were finally persuaded, against their initial beliefs, that today's Dundee is a better place. It's hard to disagree, but then this is only a postcard – you'd have to live here for a lifetime to be able to make up your own mind.

Best Wishes from an old pal of Desperate Dan.
XXX

PS: An old boat it may be, but it's definitely worth seeing!

Our Secret Spaces – Campsie Fells

David McVey

My own secret space is a stretch of burn in the Campsie Fells, green, soaring hills that rise just ten miles north of Glasgow. A popular walk to a 1,400-foot summit passes below a prominent rock outcrop topped with rowans. A branch path – narrow and easy to miss – breaks off, offering a route to a more rarely climbed 1,600-foot peak. This path goes over the outcrop, along a flat stretch of ground that is choked by thick bracken in summer, and then drops to a fast-flowing, gleaming burn. The route to the peak crosses the burn and follows a steep line of ridge to high ground. On the summit, I once met another local walker. 'Six years I've lived here,' he told me, 'and I climb this hill every week. You're the first person I've ever met on the top!'

So, few people follow the summit path, and fewer still pause where it crosses the burn, at a level of around 700 feet. Here, the burn issues from a narrow gorge thick with rowan and alder and willow. The gradient lessens, and for 100 yards it tumbles over rocks and bright beds of gravel through a shallow, treeless green glen, before plummeting again into a deep, densely wooded gorge.

Above the secret space, the ridge leading to the 1,600-foot summit seems to rise to a sharp peak – actually an illusion created by foreshortening. The immediate slopes alongside the burn are gentle and green and strewn with boulders. Sit on one of these boulders, with your back to the apparent pointed summit and the bubbling burn at your feet, and you look across a broad strath of rich farmland and small woods to another range of heathery hills that rise a mile away. Stand on the edges of the little glen and you can look north to the broad blue splash of Loch Lomond, framed by the Luss Hills on the left and Ben Lomond on the right. Look south, and, incongruously, there is the urban sprawl and tower blocks of Glasgow. Simply return to the side of the burn and the city is very far away.

This secret space is at its best in the spring. In March or April, the waters of the burn are full and at their freshest and clearest and brightest. The new grass is a blazing green, a few spring flowers bravely show themselves and there is not yet the enclosing jungle of bracken – so the approach is made easily across a flattened bed of last year's growth.

Of course, winter's footprint often lingers long into the spring, especially 700 feet up. One March day I arrived at the secret space to find the burn still in the grip of the previous night's frost. Only as I arrived did the sun rise clear of the bulk of the Campsies to the south-east. Fragile chandeliers of ice traced the spray patterns below the little waterfalls while the calmer stretches of water bubbled beneath a tight, clinging, frozen skin. As I watched, the waters below and the sunlight above combined their strength and one flat sheet of ice slowly vanished to reveal startlingly clear waters rippling over clean gravel.

I have often tried to capture the place's magic on film, but never to my own satisfaction. It is, after all, just a stretch of burn; its magic comes from something within the observer and from something in the moment. This place grows and changes and develops. On no two visits is it ever quite the same.

The colour-strewn kaleidoscope of bright gravels and gleaming pebbles beneath the shining water is always there yet constantly changing, swirled around and reapportioned by the power of the burn. Larger rocks shift and roll in times of spate, and from their revised position break the surface and trouble the flow in new ways, forming new patterns and shapes. A branch may come off a rowan upstream and lodge between two rocks, causing a major change in the burn's flow; soberingly, a sheep's skull may appear by the burnside after a hard winter; a smear of gravel can streak the grassy banks, marking the limits of an exceptional spate.

My most recent visit was on a warm but cloudy afternoon in the last days of summer. The grass and taller plants soared, high and rank, even in little dry spits of gravel in midstream, ready for the decline and decay of autumn. A few low-growing plants had already succumbed and dropped bright gold and orange leaves into still pools where they lay beside red pinpoints – rowan berries carried downstream from the upper gorge. High on the banks, some tufts of heather flamed purple. Thankfully, there was a strong warm breeze, or I may have been engulfed by clouds of terror-midges. A few sad-looking flies did cling to some flat rocks in the burn.

I've encountered few animals here – other than sheep, for the entire unforested tracts of the Campsie Fells are an extended upland sheepwalk. The odd roe deer strays in from the woods and I once saw a nippy weasel lope from one rock outcrop to another. I know dippers ply this burn – I've seen them lower down – but they have never appeared for me in the secret space, though I've encountered both grey and pied wagtails.

The screeching of pheasants echoes up from the woods, buzzards mew overhead and, in summer, wrens trill from their hidey-holes in the thick bracken. But you have to climb a bit higher on the open hill to hear curlews, meadow pipits and skylarks.

It won't be long before I return there. I'm never bored however long I sit in the sunshine and listen to the burn and the birds and the breeze. A change in the weather, a shift in the light or the mood of the sky, the endless rhythm of the seasons – this place never fails to surprise or inspire.

Park Life

James Carson

Not everyone can claim to have two palaces, four fountains, a triumphal arch and a monument to Lord Nelson on their doorstep. Well, I suppose the Queen can, but she's too busy opening hospitals and trooping colours to take much notice of her surroundings. I, on the other hand, have come to appreciate the benefits of living on the fringe of a historic park where monuments to the past rub shoulders with visions of the future.

Glasgow Green is the city's oldest public park, a space that's played a vibrant role in the life of Glasgow for over 500 years. From an early age, it made its mark on my own life too. I still remember taking my new bike down to the Green and tearing around its paths while my mammy kept up a litany of warnings: 'Mind yourself on that thing; and don't go near the road; and don't go too fast!' Twenty years later, I made my home on the edge of Glasgow Green; sixteen years on, I'm still there.

It may not have the swan boats of Boston Common or the wild deer of Phoenix Park, but there are enough unique attractions in and around Glasgow Green to divert tourists and natives alike. There's history, for a start. The land it now occupies was gifted to the people by King James II in 1450, for grazing cattle and sheep. That's a privilege still granted to those with the freedom of the city, although I've yet to stumble across Nelson Mandela flaunting his flock.

By the late 19th century, the Green had become home to the annual Glasgow Fair, a two-week trading market that evolved into a funfair, known locally as 'the shows'. I've got vivid childhood memories of the Fair. It was the only time of year I got to eat candyfloss, I always won a goldfish in the shooting gallery and it was always dead by the time I got home. The noise and colour and lights of the shows were exhilarating for a ten year old, but I never had the courage to go on anything more adventurous than the dodgems. I still don't.

The Fair is one of those occasions when the usually tranquil Glasgow Green erupts into a passable impersonation of Krakatoa. My ears are still throbbing from the 50 squillion decibels blasting out from a Michael Jackson concert on the Green in 1991. It really did seem as if he was performing inside my house – a frightening thought, even in those days. Since then, the Green has become an established venue for performers as varied as Oasis, Billy Bragg, the Stereophonics and the Drifters.

Music of a different stripe takes over each August, when Glasgow Green becomes a field of dreams for competitors in the World Pipe Band Championships. On the morning of the finals, I'm awoken by the familiar strains of 'Highland Cathedral' or 'Scotland the Brave', and for a moment I have to try and work out how I ended up at Balmoral. As the day goes on, the sound of a thousand cats being strangled becomes too much and I'm forced to retreat to somewhere just out of earshot – Belgium, usually. Then there's Bonfire Night. On November 5, excited crowds beat a path to the Green for the shock and awe of 50,000 fireworks exploding in the sky, the sound of which has been known to startle small animals in the Congo.

For many years, the Green has been a favourite spot for sporty types. Here, the harbinger of spring is not the call of the first cuckoo, but the breathless pant of the first jogger, a hardy soul who's been waiting all winter to inflict his sweatbands and Day-Glo shorts on unsuspecting doggy-walkers. It's here too that the tape is broken at the end of the city's major road races. If Glasgow's bid for the Commonwealth Games is successful, the Green will play host to the egg and spoon events. And yes, I made that last bit up.

The eastern section of the Green, known as Fleshers' Haugh, had its own 15 minutes of fame in 1745, when Bonnie Prince Charlie reviewed his troops there before the ill-fated Battle of Culloden. Today, it's home to the Glasgow Football Centre, a massive complex of 18 grass and synthetic pitches that replaced the muddy terrain which grazed many a Glaswegian knee. I took a stroll over there one Saturday afternoon, just as two teams had temporarily abandoned their match to indulge in the traditional Scottish pastime of decapitating the referee. This was far more entertaining than football, and I have to say that if Scottish teams put as much passion into our national game as this lot did into terrorising the unfortunate arbiter, they might have a greater chance of beating the likes of Bhutan and Equatorial Guinea. Luckily for the ref, the sound and fury was brief, and the teams went back to the equally traditional pastime of knocking seven bells out of each other.

Athletic pursuits on Glasgow Green aren't confined to the land. The city's rowing clubs use a stretch of the River Clyde that flows through the park for training and competitions. The river is one of the Green's great natural features, especially since tougher pollution controls have made it cleaner. Not so long ago, your only chance of seeing a salmon in Glasgow was either on a tin or on the city's coat of arms. But they've now returned to the Clyde, along with herons, kingfishers and seals. Spanning the river at this point, and connecting Glasgow Green with the south side is the small, but perfectly formed, St Andrew's Suspension Bridge. Built in 1855, its extravagant columns and royal blue livery make this bridge a bonnie link across the Clyde. In fact (and you should have been expecting this) it's bonnie and Clyde.

The Green in itself is a pleasant space to explore, but in and around the park there are local landmarks that make a visit here all the more enjoyable. These days, an establishment with the name of 'the People's Palace' might evoke images of a trendy restaurant in Warsaw or a snazzy new headquarters for the Labour Party. But this People's Palace is a museum that tells the story of our city. In 1898, the Earl of Rosebery declared it 'open for ever and ever'. And so it has remained. Except when it's closed, of course.

Inside the elegant, domed building, visitors can trace Glasgow's story from its earliest days to the present. All aspects of the city's life are featured, from housing and work to entertainment and sport. Glasgow's radical tradition is evoked by banners recalling causes that generations of citizens rallied to – trade unions, votes for women, the Spanish Civil War, the miners' strike. Many of these rallies took place on Glasgow Green, which is still a gathering place for political protest. As recently as 2003, 80,000 people assembled here to voice their opposition to the war in Iraq.

On the upper floors of the People's Palace, there are full-size recreations of a one-roomed tenement from the old Gorbals district, a Second World War bomb shelter and the oft-lamented Glasgow wash house – the 'steamie'. There's also a diverting section devoted to the almost impenetrable Glasgow dialect. It's entertaining to observe visitors from Brisbane and California watching a video of Stanley Baxter's *Parliamo Glasgow* sketch, as they try to work out what 'Wherra-helza-booze' could possibly mean.

Recently, the People's Palace hosted an exhibition of snapshots taken in the Glasgow of 1955. The photographs were absorbing – a production line at the old Albion lorries plant, women doing their washing at the steamie – but just as revealing were the comments written by visitors to the exhibition:

I have mixed memories about the steamies. I had to do my mother's washing while she stood and blethered.

And this from a British Columbia resident:

We left Glasgow in 1975. Not a day goes by when we don't think about this majestic old city.

Tacked on to the back of the museum is its very own Crystal Palace – the Winter Gardens. The glass shell of this impressive botanical garden is said to replicate the upturned hull of HMS *Victory*, Nelson's flagship. There's a nice little café here, where you can have soup and a sandwich, or you can promenade amidst the palm trees and tropical plants from Africa and South America. The Winter Gardens have also become a popular venue for wedding receptions; I've sometimes drifted off to sleep at night as the first strains of 'Agadoo' waft across the Green. Talk about the stuff of nightmares.

In 2005, the People's Palace got a new neighbour – no less than Her Britannic Majesty, Queen Victoria. She stands now, glaring at the building from her perch on top of the world's largest terracotta fountain. Gifted to the city by Sir Henry Doulton for the 1888 International Exhibition, the fountain was moved to Glasgow Green in 1890. A century later, it was showing signs of serious neglect, but help was at hand from the National Lottery – proof that gambling isn't always such a bad thing. Now beautifully restored, the Doulton Fountain is a striking remnant of old Empire. Beneath Victoria, her peoples are depicted in their working clothes – Australians rearing sheep, Canadians with a dead moose and smartly dressed Indians looking slightly embarrassed to be part of such a confection.

As if the Doulton Fountain weren't dazzling enough, just a few feet away there's another dramatic feast for the eyes. The Templeton Building was modelled on the Doge's Palace in Venice, and you'll be hard pressed to find a more startling architectural statement anywhere else in Glasgow. Red, gold and green bricks zigzag across its Byzantine facade, like something that's sprung from the mind of a modern-day Gaudí. In fact, it's the creation of a Victorian architect, William Leiper. But while he might have known all about designing an attention-seeking building, unfortunately Leiper didn't care much for little matters like health and safety. Its construction was nearing completion when the untethered façade crashed onto the factory behind. Twenty-nine young women were killed.

Time was when the Templeton factory made carpets destined for places like the White House, and the Taj Mahal. But times and tastes change; these days the White House is probably kitted out in parquet flooring by Linda Barker and the Taj Mahal likely has Tibetan rugs from IKEA. Meanwhile, the Templeton factory closed in 1982, and during the Thatcher years it was given new life as a business centre. In another sign of the times, it's now being converted to luxury apartments and penthouses.

Almost lost beside this current construction site, there's a breath of the mystic east (and I don't mean Edinburgh). The James Martin Fountain has an exotic canopy with a Moorish style about it. The fountain honours a Glasgow councillor who dedicated his life to affordable housing for the working-class poor. Maybe it's just me, but I could swear the fountain is tilting away from its yuppie neighbours.

Further evidence of the Green's changing face can be seen on its western flank. The Homes for the Future project is one of the tangible legacies of Glasgow's year as the UK City of Architecture and Design in 1999. Architects from near and far were selected to design this ground-breaking complex, and the result is a curious mixture of cubes, curves, timber and copper. Oh, and if this development is anything to go by, the future's not orange – it's white. The buildings are futuristic in function as well as form: underfloor insulation and solar panels have been installed in the apartments, which have been selling for six-figure sums. All of which will ensure that this part of the dear, green place lives up to its name.

The Homes for the Future complex is a very far cry from my own humble hovel in Monteith Row, which overlooks the Green's northern perimeter. But what it lacks in style, this little terrace makes up for in pedigree. It was named after Henry Monteith, the city's Lord Provost, at the beginning of the 19th century. Its handsome town houses attracted well-heeled residents of the time, including James Templeton (of carpet factory fame). But as Glasgow's centre of gravity shifted west, Monteith Row fell on hard times, and the mansions made way for tenements to house the influx of new workers surging into the city.

Today, a 1980s housing development occupies Monteith Row, and all that remains of the original terrace is a solitary building at the western end. A sign advertises it as the Monteith

Hotel, but this particular establishment isn't part of the Hilton empire. It's a lodging house for the homeless, and a reminder that Glasgow Green is located in the city's East End, an area that could cover itself in glory if poverty indicators won Olympic events. From high crime and low incomes to poor health and drug abuse, it's here that Glasgow's post-industrial image of a style centre and cultural capital comes unstuck. The Monteith Hotel is a couple of minutes and a million light years from the Homes for the Future.

Early photographs of Glasgow show a triumphal arch dominating that part of the Green now facing the Monteith Hotel. But the arch isn't there any more, and it's not even where it was moved to next. In fact, the McLennan Arch is one of the most peripatetic bits of masonry you're likely to find – if you can find it. It was the only part of James and Robert Adam's Glasgow Assembly Rooms to survive demolition, and was taken, stone by stone from the city centre to its first home on the Green in 1822. Later, it turned up at the park's Charlotte Street entrance, before finally settling down at its present location – the Saltmarket, which is Glasgow Green's most westerly point. Presumably the Arch's wandering days are done, but I haven't ruled out the possibility of coming home one night to find it parked outside my front door.

The McLennan Arch may have been an early monumental feature of Glasgow Green, but it wasn't the first. That distinction rests with the obelisk which now dominates the central section of the park. Built in 1806, it's the first civic monument anywhere to honour Admiral Lord Nelson. Having survived lightning strikes and years of neglect, the newly restored obelisk has been another beneficiary of Lottery funding that has transformed the landscape of Glasgow Green. From this point, amidst the trees and beautifully kept lawns, there's a fantastic view of Glasgow's skyline: the towers of the City Chambers and the 340-year-old pagoda-like Merchants' Steeple jockey for space with the modern buildings of Strathclyde University and the UGC cinema – voted Scotland's ugliest building before it had even opened.

And now, here comes the science: in 1765, close to the spot where the Nelson obelisk now stands, the inventor James Watt conceived the idea of the separate condenser. Which might not mean much to you or me (especially me), but it was this moment of inspiration that dramatically improved the efficiency of steam engines, a development that would revolutionise manufacturing and turn Glasgow into the workshop of the world. The stone next to the obelisk marks the spot where Watt had his Eureka moment and is inscribed with the date when the Industrial Revolution was born.

It may be 16 summers since I took up residence next to Glasgow Green, but it's a bailiwick that still has the capacity to surprise. Only recently, I discovered the existence of the Glasgow Police Museum, located just behind the Homes for the Future complex. It's a real treasure house, jam-packed with artifacts that tell the story of Britain's oldest police force. Displays include early uniforms, with top hats and elaborately decorated truncheons that look more like rolling pins. Another room's walls are covered with police badges and insignia from all nations – even the Vatican is represented. Unexpectedly, there's also a plaque designed by Charles Rennie Mackintosh – his first paid commission. Mackintosh's father was a police superintendent, and he made sure junior got the job of designing this sculpture to honour a senior colleague. The modest piece is unremarkable, but there are hints in the Celtic designs of the unique style that would later make Mackintosh and his city world famous.

The police museum is located close to one of my favourite buildings in Glasgow – St Andrew's Church. Completed in 1739, its slender clock tower and massive portico are said to be reminiscent of St Martin's in the Field in London, but as with the Doge's Palace, I'd say Glasgow got the better deal. In the year 2000, the building was restored to its pre-Victorian glory and became a centre for traditional Scottish music and dance. It might no longer be a church, but inside, Corinthian columns and fine plasterwork testify that the divine influence hasn't abandoned this beautiful building.

Watching the faces of Glaswegian visitors to that photographic exhibition in the People's Palace, I was struck by their responses. Many were bewildered to see how much their city has changed in only 50 years. Parts of Glasgow have been torn asunder, whole streets have disappeared and many of our most beautiful buildings have been lost forever. On Glasgow Green, there have been changes too, but they have been mostly for the better. The bits worth keeping are being preserved, while room is being made for new developments to attract future generations. As for me, my long-time association with this lovely park means it will always be the green, green grass of home. One of my mammy's favourite sayings was 'Never forget where you came from.' Well, there's not much chance of that; it's hard to forget where you came from when you've never really left.

A Magical History Tour of Edinburgh

Susan Mansfield

Even stones have a story to tell, written on their surface, saturated with veins and sediments. All you have to do is look at them and they will tell of their centuries–old existence.

Aurora Fonda

This profusion of eccentricities, this dream in masonry and living rock is not a drop scene in a theatre, but a city in a world of reality.

Robert Louis Stevenson

I. Second from the Left

There's nothing like seven storeys of 1960s concrete for obscuring a perfectly good view. The second gargoyle from the left on the north-facing wall of Trinity College Apse feels this acutely. Once, he scowled proudly from the parapet of one of Edinburgh's finest Gothic churches. Now he's squeezed unceremoniously between a stern Evangelical meeting hall and the back of Jurys Inn, which is even now disgorging American tourists into the mouth of Chalmers Close.

Still, it's better than sitting on a pile of rocks on Calton Hill for 30 years with your gob open and your legs in a permanent crouch. The gargoyle knows this too. Beautiful, ornate Trinity College Church, founded by Mary of Gueldres in 1460 in memory of her husband King James II, was demolished in the 19th century to make room for a railway siding. The stones were numbered with the intent to rebuild, but as the years passed and the authorities argued, many were pilfered; medieval carvings became garden ornaments all over the city. The gargoyle was lucky. He lasted to see the apse rebuilt to the south of Jeffrey Street, accompanied by a Victorian church which was levelled in 1960.

Today the apse is a Brass Rubbing Centre. It could be worse. The house of Archbishop Spottiswoode is the back end of a pub. On the High Street the old frontages house a bookmakers, a PDSA shop and various purveyors of tartan and postcards blasting out techno bagpipe music into the cobbled street. There's no point being proud. If you're made of stone you can afford to take the long view.

In the stones of Edinburgh, the past compacts like sediment, buried for a time, but never removed. It took the Old Town fire of December 2002 to reveal the extent to which old Edinburgh was built on, and in some cases from, older Edinburgh. Stones found new uses, closes changed their course, ancient spaces full of memories were shut off in the foundations of newer buildings to be reopened on a future day. The fire uncovered stones as old as the city itself.

At the same time, as the gargoyle well knows, age is no guarantee of status. And status matters in this split-level, upstairs-downstairs city. Contained by the ancient city walls the Old Town grew in the only direction it could – vertically. Ad lib constructions became so haphazard that Dickens compared them to houses of cards. The gargoyle hears the rattle of teacups through the open window of the Rabbie Burns Café, catches the eye of a haughty black cat on an upper windowsill, glances longingly towards the graceful arches of Old St Pauls, and knows he's been relegated to the cheap seats. It's possible to go down in the world in Edinburgh without moving even an inch.

II. The Shoemaker of Peace

It's busy, busy, busy down in the Canongate since the new Parliament opened. Many more pairs of feet every day, thundering past the Shoemaker of Peace without so much as a backward glance. However, if you care to stop at the doorway of 185 Canongate (bought by the Guild of Shoemakers in 1677) you'll find him carved in stone solemnly indicating an open book with a biblical rhyme:

> *Behold how good a thing it is*
> *and how becoming well,*
> *Together such as brothers are*
> *in unity to dwell.*

'It is an honour,' it concludes, 'for men to cease from strife.' It's a message delivered without undue ceremony, by a man who knew the value of a good pair of soles. He might have the wings of a cherub, but he has the face of a Canongate shoemaker.

The Shoemaker looks down at the faces: tourists training their lenses on the Tolbooth, Parliamentary fixers yapping into mobile phones, students from Moray House College jogging with their iPods, and considers the state of their footwear: trainers and brogues, pumps and stilettos, all being worn out on the unforgiving streets of Edinburgh as their owners try to cover more ground just a little bit faster.

It doesn't surprise him that there's no time for a message like his in this talking shop of a town. Edinburgh always preferred ideas to industry: a city of lawyers and bankers and university men, the birthplace of the Enlightenment. Talk, talk, talk. And then there were the quiet, pragmatic conversations among powerful men in mansions barely a stone's throw from this spot. Men who sealed Scotland's participation in the Treaty of Union ceding our Parliament to the control of Westminster.

Now, nearly 300 years later, that particular conversation has been reopened. A new elected body sits in Enric Miralles' confusing homage to democracy at the bottom of the hill. The Shoemaker hopes that they might notice, as they shuttle to and fro, his message about honour and strife. He hopes they keep their feet on the ground.

III. The Angel in the Back Row

It's safest not to ask the angel above the main door of Lady Glenorchy's Parish Church for her opinion on this point. Unquestionably, it would be withering. She has the wings of a celestial body, but the face of a jowly Edinburgh matron who's stepped in something malodorous. That's the trouble with philanthropy. It requires mingling with those who are not our sort of people.

Lady Glenorchy founded her relief mission to the Old Town poor in 1770, a time when there was no shortage of good needing done. She was long dead when her showpiece non-denominational church was demolished to make way for Waverley Station. After much strife, the congregation found new premises on Roxburgh Place, part of an ancient thoroughfare known as Back Row, taking the good lady's remains with them.

When the rebuilt church opened its doors in 1913, the angel

found she was closer than she cared to be to the grimy tenements of St Leonards and Dumbiedykes, rife with squalour and disease. Down the road, a philanthropic Trust had taken over the disused brewery at 60 The Pleasance pledging to 'bring light and air and beauty into Pleasance daily life.' Amenities would eventually include a gynamsium, play hall, bathrooms, coffee room, and a Violet Ray Room where malnourished tenement children were stretched out to bask in the 'perpetual sunlight' of 'pure' ultraviolet rays.

Fifty years later, the tenements were gone and the families rehoused in new tower-block estates on the periphery. Church attendance dropped, even in Lady Glenorchy's, once the busiest church in Edinburgh, and the congregation merged with the remnant from Trinity College Church and moved to Wester Hailes, taking their founder to her fifth (and one hopes final) resting place.

The church was bought by Edinburgh University, as was 60 The Pleasance, and both became venues for the burgeoning Festival Fringe. For 30 years, Lady Glenorchy's served as an exam hall, but is now a privately owned all-year-round arts venue, the Roxy Art House. The angel likes it little better, but there's no pleasing some people. She is no longer consulted.

IV. The Wounded Deer

Some parts of the body you miss more than others, according to the hind that lives on the West Bow Well. She is missing parts of all four of her legs, but that's no great hardship when you don't intend going anywhere. She still has her head, unlike the maiden holding up the other side of the city shield. She may have lost part of her nose, but down here that's no bad thing.

Down here, where the Cowgate meets the Grassmarket,

you're in the bowels of the city and no mistake. For centuries it was the principal livestock market, and you know what happens when a lot of cattle get anxious in a confined space. In any case, in the gardez-loo era, when out of the window meant out of mind, you quickly learned that liquid runs downhill, and this is about as far down as you can get. The stench had a life of its own, the houses swarming with so much overcrowded life that they seem to breathe all by themselves.

The story of this area is of discontent, drunkenness, riots, executions and other forms of street theatre. Plenty of lives ended on the Grassmarket gallows – murderers, witches, petty crooks, folk who were in the wrong place at the wrong time. Covenanters, those who dared to make their own pact with God to defy a Papish king, were marched down from the prison created for them in Greyfriars and hung ten to a scaffold before being dragged back up and dumped in a pauper's grave. The hind has seen all this, has seen too much.

West Bow Well was built in 1674, part of the city's ambitious plan to bring fresh water to the old town. More often, the authorities simply swept the problems under the carpet. Later generations would build bridges over the lower eschelons of the city and develop the properties on the upper level. Once an underground street infested with plague was simply walled off and forgotten. Millionaire Andrew Carnegie swept in with the dollars to fund the new Central Library, but you can bet he wasn't told that its feet are in the Cowgate. Edinburgh can be a two-faced town.

In the 20th century, slum clearance eased the overcrowding, and the lower sections of the Old Town became the preserve of dosshouses and second-hand shops. With the worst poverty gone, the area became positively bohemian. When the avant-garde rolled into Edinburgh in the 1960s like a long-delayed train, it was here that it found a home in the Traverse Theatre, moving from its first home, in an old brothel in the Lawnmarket, to West Bow in 1968.

Today down is the new up. The Traverse has moved on, rebuilt, rebranded. The old theatre has been turned into flats. There are new glass-fronted hotels and the second-hand shops sell 'retro fashion' for students from the art college. The damp, forgotten, lower floors of the Central Library have been turned into a thriving Fringe venue.

The drunkenness, however, remains. Whether the hind lost her appendages a hundred years ago or in last week's stag parties is anyone's guess. Sometimes, she thinks, the only thing that has changed is the colour of the pavement pizzas. Then again, at least these days no one gets killed.

V. His Beloved Maida

It's one of the great icons of Edinburgh, perhaps the greatest after the Castle, but the Scott Monument is the source of some bemusement. When you get up close to this 200-feet high piece of sandstone confectionery to see what it's all about, you find seated at the base a writer and his dog: Sir Walter Scott and his beloved Maida.

She lies at his side gazing up at him devotedly. Of course sculptors look at everything through rose-tinted glasses. But Maida knows a thing or two. Like the fact that people don't get 200-foot memorials within 12 years of their death just for being a talented writer.

No, it's a whole lot more complex than that. Scott was an Edinburgh man, ambitious for his city. He was well connected, a mover and shaker, he wanted to put Edinburgh on the map. In 1822 he got his chance with the visit of King George IV, the first by a reigning monarch to Scotland since 1650. He managed all 'twenty-one daft days' like a theatrical director, with the city as the stage and backdrop. With a neo-classical New Town proclaimed the Athens of the North, and an Old Town steeped in romance and history (as long as you watched where you were putting your feet), he couldn't fail. The English aristocracy began a love affair with Scotland which would last for the best part of a century.

Alright, so he took a few liberties along the way, like the introduction of tartan, previously associated with renegades and Jacobites, as the country's national dress. The portly monarch himself even donned a kilt and gave the caricaturists enough material to last for months.

But Scott understood the power of myth, and so does Maida. Why else would it be that she gets barely a photograph while tourists are queuing up to be snapped with the scrappy little Skye terrier up at Greyfriars? Maida doubts it was selfless devotion that kept him coming back to the graveyard for 14 years. More likely his celebrity guaranteed him meals at the nearby coffee house. Or perhaps it was the more base attraction of any dog to a piece of ground saturated with bones. But one mustn't let the truth get in the way of a good legend.

When Sir Walter and Maida took their places on the plinth in 1844, Princes Street was the envy of Europe. Henry James himself would say as much. They have watched in silence as the grand houses gave way to 1960s chain stores. And, in the best street in town, fortunes still fluctuate: Jenners bought out by House of Fraser and upstaged by Harvey Nichols, M&S losing out to H&M.

Now as the day ends, they watch the faces of Edinburgh hurry past them: tired-eyed office workers clutching TV dinners, Ozzie backpackers with the world in their rucksacks, weary tourists returning to their identical rooms in Jurys Inn, revellers spruced up in search of a good time. The streetlights come on and the floodlights make a halo around the Castle in the evening mist. It is what Stevenson might have recognised as an Edinburgh moment, one in which you pinch yourself to remember that this is 'not a drop scene in a theatre, but a city in a world of reality.'

Sailing Through the Heavens

Michael T.R.B. Turnbull

I was born in February 1941 at the American Hospital in Istanbul. My Scots father had been forced to break his circuitous journey: he was on his way with my mother from Liverpool to Stockholm – via South Africa, Egypt and the Holy Land – to coordinate Special Operations Executive activities in Denmark and Norway. From Istanbul he and my young Brazilian mother and her newborn son took the last Russian ship across the Black Sea to Odessa, then by train up to Moscow and a flight a day later through snow and sunshine to Sweden. After the War we settled in Copenhagen but in 1945 my mother died in a freak car accident. My father reluctantly left the Foreign Office and took me across the Atlantic to the tropical warmth of my Brazilian grandparents' house overlooking Botafogo Bay in sunny Rio de Janeiro. He remarried not long after. I proved to be a handful for my young stepmother and so was sent north to live with my Scottish grandparents in Edinburgh.

In the autumn of 1948 I left Brazil on a British South American Airways York airliner (a modification of the Lancaster bomber), flying out of Rio bound for London – via Recife on the north-east coast of Brazil, Dakar in French West

Africa and Lisbon. Still clutching my worn but much-loved teddy bear, (which had come with me from Sweden), I was taken into the cockpit by the stewardess and then allowed to stand inside the Perspex astrodome, gazing at the stars high above and the ribbed sands of the Sahara rushing past not so far below.

After spending the night in Lisbon, we landed in London where my grandfather met me. He was a stocky, gruff ex-Indian Army colonel with a walrus moustache. He looked with amusement at the old-fashioned tweed plus-fours my father had made me wear.

The train journey north from London was not particularly happy. My grandfather said very little. I said even less. From time to time I shut myself into the toilet where I sang mournful Brazilian songs. 'Where am I going?' I thought to myself.

Edinburgh was a culture shock. Princes Street was full of little old ladies tightly wrapped in dark-brown coats. It was like Soviet Russia. My grandparents and my unmarried aunt lived in a substantial semidetached stone house in Church Hill, a quiet side street at the heart of douce Morningside. Grandfather's family had originally been Border farmers so he had an inborn love of the soil. Retired and now a senior bailie on the town council, he was in charge of Edinburgh's parks and gardens. Our own garden was a thing of beauty, full of tall blue delphiniums, roses and other flowers of every colour. Passers-by regularly stopped by the green wooden gate to admire the magnificent floral displays.

My grandparents' home was comfortable but regimented. On the walls hung fragrant watercolours of Kashmir and the house was full of strange objects which my grandfather had brought back from the Sikkim Tibet Mission of 1904 – a frightening red wooden ritual mask; a leather shield, an enormous three-part copper trumpet and a hollow silver goddess with eight arms which for many years presided enigmatically over my bedroom.

My grandmother was a woman of wide reading. She played the piano and loved the German language. On her shoulders (and those of her mother) had been the responsibility of bringing up her four children during the frequent long periods when my grandfather was with the Army in India.

Neither my grandmother nor my grandfather found it easy to express their feelings in public. My grandfather had been responsible for physical education in the Indian Army and also trained the Indian hockey team which won a gold medal at the 1928 Olympics. He had a good baritone voice and enjoyed singing dramatic and humorous ballads. Apart from tending his garden his great delight was collecting stamps which he kept in a locked wooden roll-top desk in his study. After his death I discovered a Freemason's regalia neatly folded inside a small brown suitcase in his study.

Family life in Scotland was suitably vigorous with walks and outings to the countryside being an important feature. It was also strictly controlled. Meal times were announced by the deep booming of a polished black and gold Tibetan gong which hung at the foot of the stairs. For me, the biggest contrast between Brazil and Edinburgh was the change from fried steak, rice, beans and colourful fruit salads to mince, boiled potatoes and steamed puddings!

Christmas, with its warm family conviviality, made up, to some degree, for the barrenness of the Edinburgh winter. Our family assembled from various parts of Britain and abroad, strangers at first, but gradually rediscovering a common bond amid slices of turkey and funny hats. After crackers had been pulled and toasts drunk, charades followed. Presents were exchanged under the Christmas tree which glittered with candles, shining balls and tinsel.

On New Year's Day came the first-foots carrying tangerines or a bottle. Then, on Twelfth Night, the carnival atmosphere ended when the tree and all the cards were taken down and the decorations packed away.

When the time came I was sent to boarding school. My first Scottish school (Blynlee) was in Galashiels. It was more a home than a school and was run by a husband and wife, who provided a warm and supportive imitation of family living. Although the school was coeducational, the girls were treated differently only in so far as they had separate dormitories. They played rounders with us, sat on the green wooden seesaw and helped us in the treasure hunts organised by the headmaster and his wife. The headmaster baked wonderful cakes late into the night, made armies of brightly coloured puppets and even built a model railway to entertain us. Each child put the sweets received from home into a large blue tin which we were all allowed to dip into twice a week – subtly teaching us the value of sharing.

By conducting chemical experiments before our very eyes he filled us with a mania for science. He introduced us to the riches of reading. Once a week, in the long dark evenings of winter, we listened to the detective radio series, 'Dick Barton'. It fuelled our imagination even more.

There was a large garden around the school house and a hill above it which was ploughed for turnips. That was the field where, spurred by a fascination for archaeology, we went to look for prehistoric arrowheads. Sometimes the headmaster drove us down to the town on shopping expeditions. For a special treat we could sit in the curious seat in the open boot of the car and wave to passers-by like royalty.

Then, inexplicably, the school closed and we were all shifted to another establishment in town. Here, we could sense that our new headmaster was less interested in children. He was a busy extrovert, unlike his bookish predecessor. We scarcely saw him and he did not exert the same influence on our imagination and feelings as the 'home' school. Yet there were some new and special pleasures. Every fortnight we could ride a small white pony or a tall chestnut mare. In the corner of the garden was a pond which had an air of mystery about it because of the many toy submarines that had sunk into the unfathomable depths of its muddy bottom.

During the long summer holidays my aunt and grandmother took us to a small holiday cottage at Nethybridge half-hidden by bushes and trees. Down the road were long stretches of fields. I dreamed of that place at night. Below our cottage was a berry bush. Whenever we passed along that road a small white horse laid its gentle head over the hedge. It was timid but warm and strong to the touch.

There my friends and I played in the neighbouring fields, tearing up the turf heavy with the dark-brown earth, dropping it into the small stream to form a dam. Our wellington boots sank below the level of the water with a satisfying squelch, so we pulled them off and just waded with bare feet and legs. Down that road were stretches of fields. In the late summer the farmers would begin the harvest. I had never seen a cornfield before or a haystack or a combine-harvester. There I saw my first sheep, cows and pigs.

I loved the green bushes, the brambles and the flowers of all species, the towering pines and firs. Further along the road outside our cottage was what I was told had been an old prisoner-of-war camp, deserted now but still with its barbed wire, pieces of rusty machinery, piles of sawdust and a peat bog.

Next to the camp was an old half-collapsed house, its garden overgrown but still full of roses, briars and nettles. We heard that a witch had lived there. Our mouths dry with fear, we explored the house, creeping through the littered rooms. In the garden was a locked shed. Inside we could see odd pieces of furniture and other much more mysterious shapes.

Other summers we stayed a few miles away at Grantown with its ruined Castle Grant, out of which enormous trees sprouted. My grand-uncle lived at the edge of the town. We fished in the stream, guddling with our hands, and catching small trout with our fingers by stroking them as they lay hidden under stones. There were cows in the field from which we took warm white milk and, beyond, another pasture in which we found, embedded in the uneven grass, striped red and grey mortar bombs. There were said to be wild cats on the slopes of the hill above the river. Once we found a lair with the skeleton of a cat. Sometimes we caught glimpses of frightened does and harts flying gracefully to the cover of the trees.

The most exciting part of our time in Morayshire was the Highland Games: hammer-throwing, highland dancing, bicycle races, sheepdog trials and tossing the caber. The Games were a living relic of an age when the community was agricultural, transport slower and landowners and gentry had greater influence. It was a moment of anarchy and passion to celebrate the fruitfulness of the land.

Two years after arriving in Scotland I was sent to a boarding school on the east coast at North Berwick. While my aunt and grandmother sat in the headmaster's study I walked through the grounds. I came upon a group of boys laughing and cheering in the woods. They were dancing round a low henhut made of wood and chicken wire in which a boy struggled. He had been gagged and tied hand and foot.

I was accepted and soon found myself a member of the 60-strong school population. As the weeks passed our high spirits were curbed by the teachers. No running in the corridor, no reading in bed once the lights were out, no shouting, no swearing and no laughter except at breaks and recreation. It was the custom for good conduct points to be awarded to each house. Points were also deducted for bad behaviour. When the points were assessed at the end of each week, the heads of each house would announce a ritual punishment on the grapevine for those who had more conspicuously tarnished their house's record. Down into the woods the hounds tracked their quarry. Then the culprits were flung into beds of nettles and beaten with broken branches.

I came to know gangs at school. One's conduct as a member of, for example, the Black Hand Gang, was strictly regulated by a complex set of rules and punishments. Gang fights were part of life. Two or three boys would collect followers and build a den in the woods. There they held court, dispensed favours and passed judgement. Periodically, war would be declared on a rival gang. The thought of a battle hung brooding in the truce period of a class or a school meal until the free time when hostilities erupted. No quarter was given (or expected). The gang economy produced a servile state where beds had to be made for punishment, shoes polished or a tribute of sweets exacted. Woe betide any boy who told the staff. A clipe would be beaten even harder by his fellows. Our gangs fought dogged campaigns in the woods or among the sand dunes nearby.

Assembled at our stockade, the lookout posted up the trees, we close the drawbridge and wait for the enemy assault. At first, nothing. A long silence. Suddenly a stone whizzes through the air propelled by ink-stained fingers. It crashes through the branches overhead. Then arrows follow with deadly inaccuracy. Finally, the assault itself: masked figures wearing protective clothing and an assortment of metallic headgear. With equal ferocity we repel the enemy after many a fierce hand-to-hand struggle.

One moonlit night we raided the school tuckshop, sneaking outside, creeping across the flowerbed. We hoisted ourselves onto the open windowsill. Once inside there was complete quiet. We looked around: boxes of sweets everywhere. Working quickly we helped ourselves as the moon streamed through. We ate a few sweets then we were outside into the woods where we buried whole boxes to be unearthed and eaten later. Minutes afterwards, we were back in our dormitories.

There were also moments of light relief. At the end of each summer term came Prize Day. After the speeches, the school song and the gymnastic display, tea would be served in a giant marquee which had been set up in front of the lawn. As parents swopped pleasantries with the staff, greedy little fingers would be wriggling through the joins in the canvas. An astonished mother sinking crimson lips into a cream-puff would see a whole plate-load of eclairs and salmon sandwiches disappear before her eyes.

Crazes would sweep through the narrow confines of the school. One was for parachutes made out of handkerchiefs from which hung a small aluminium canister about the size of a photographic spool filled with soil. We wrapped the tin in the handkerchief, hurling it vertically as far as we could and then basked in the magic of its gentle descent to earth.

During the holidays, at home again in Edinburgh, my friends and I erected voluminous tents in the garden with sheets propped up on bamboo canes taken from my grandfather's garden hut. We imagined ourselves camping among the Indian hills where my grandfather had marched and struggled and dreamed. On rainy days we acted plays and charades. Using the old Victorian cut-out characters and theatrical sets which Robert Louis Stevenson had thrilled to before us, we staged the plays on tables draped with heavy tartan rugs in each other's houses. On days when we really felt the lure of the footlight we smeared Leichner stage make-up on our faces, dressed up in old costumes and borrowed one of my grandfather's dress swords. Then, mounted on bicycles, with silver-painted cardboard helmets on our heads, we swerved along the ancient lanes and leafy side streets frightening the life out of elderly ladies and children who happened to be passing.

Our house was filled with the toys of previous generations, many designed to be of educational value. I played with them without quite understanding how they worked – a magic lantern with hand-painted slides of comic figures and storms at sea. When I turned it on, its black tin frame quickly grew hot from the candle inside and puffed smoke. There was a wooden box full of games: bone spillikins, tiddlywinks, lead soldiers and a backgammon board. I rolled the old family yo-yo up and down, whipped a diavolo and almost mastered the intricacies of cup and ball. But one by one, I lost them all – even the solitaire board and the marbles with their whorls of multicoloured glass. Once or twice we came across rather weird musical instruments: an ocarina (shaped like a pear); a kazoo (shiny and noisy); an 18th-century serpent, leather-covered. I would pull out the long copper Tibetan prayer horn in the hall to its three extensions, poke it out through the front door and snarl out at the neighbours, shattering the genteel peacefulness with the bellows of an enraged bull elephant.

Every year my aunt took me to the circus in Princes Street deep in the bowels of the Waverley Market. The ring, the sawdust, the crack of the whip, the thudding of horses' hooves, spangles, tinsel and hilarious slapstick – these provided the climactic thrills of the evening's entertainment. A visit to the circus presented me and my friends with a richly textured cosmos: the bareback riders and the animal-tamers were heroes, and the clowns the simple buffoons of the underworld – but the aerialists were angels and golden gods, sailing through the heavens.

Mrs McGuffie's Knickers
(Retail Therapy)

June G. Ritchie

Mrs McGuffie sold knickers. Real knickers. Thick dark-blue gym knickers that were so cosy in the winter and so uncomfortable in the summer. To a child growing up in a small town near the Scottish Borders in the 50s, seasons were proper seasons.

In the summer, we would stuff our skirts into these copious garments when paddling in the burn or standing in a water-filled basin in the garden. In the winter, they were an excellent if albeit temporary sledge if your wee brother had borrowed your home-made wooden toboggan. They also kept your bum warm as you rattled down the hill at ferocious speeds, usually hurtling into the fence at the foot.

Most of the female inhabitants shopped at Mrs McGuffie's as she sold a wide variety of ladies' unmentionables and genteel accoutrements. They would queue quietly with decorum as befitted a ladies' outfitter and explain their needs to the discreet shopkeeper. However, in a small town there were few secrets and it was common knowledge who wore knee-length, oyster-toned bloomers and who had ordered a set of shell-pink, silk underwear garments, edged in champagne lace. Mrs McGuffie could locate any article with amazing accuracy. How did she know which unlabelled fawn cardboard box held those mysterious, stiff, shiny, beige, crackling objects worn by certain ladies in order to attain a more slimline silhouette?

Each request, whether it was for ordinary socks or expensive satin petticoats was treated with the same serious consideration. Liberty bodices were given the respect as delicate chemises; woolly mittens were allotted the same importance as a pair of white lace summer gloves.

In order to obtain the desired item, certain manoeuvres were necessary. First, a wooden stepladder was placed beside the appropriate shelf, then the proprietress herself (she had no assistants) would carefully climb up to one of the many identical boxes. Mrs McGuffie was thin, probably due to the exercise afforded by the constant use of her ladder. She wore thick grey stockings that wrinkled slightly at the ankle and shiny brown brogues. Sometimes she wore woollen fawn-coloured hose. Descending with the container tucked under one arm, she would place it on the counter and slowly, from layers of white tissue paper, extract the desired object. It would be scrutinised and, if satisfied, the customer would nod her head and begin to examine her purse. Then the lengthy process of wrapping the purchase would begin. First, strong brown paper was pulled from a roll fastened to one side of the counter and the garment would be carefully folded into this rain and windproof covering. This paper was later recycled as schoolbook covers by postwar, ration-minded mothers. Then thick fibrous string was securely tied round the parcel. A small piece was formed into a loop to facilitate transportation. The next customer would have to wait as Mrs McGuffie replaced the box and tidied up, then the whole process would begin again.

If finances allowed, the Thistle Tea Rooms beckoned and

their three-tiered cake stands awaited tired and hungry customers. We children were never allowed to begin at the top
layer where creamy meringues awaited. We had to start on the
lower plate where boring meat-paste sandwiches sulked and
then on to the middle plate with its bulky scones. Only once
you had stuffed yourself with these filling homebakes were you
free to relish your fluffy cake. By then, however, the need to
sink your teeth into its succulent sweetness had lessened.

Children had milky, sugary tea to drink. Lemonade was
considered too much of a celebratory beverage to quaff in a
tearoom but it was allowed at weddings or parties. Children's
Christmas parties were held in the Corn Exchange, a building
situated at the top of the High Street. Games that involved the
participation of every child were the main source of amusement. These included 'Farmer's in his Den', 'Be Baw Babitty'
and 'the Grand Olde Duke of York' and were enjoyed by all
ages. Music was supplied by a piano. Refreshments such as
sandwiches and home-made cakes were eagerly consumed. No
one fussed over food. If you were hungry you ate. If you were
not hungry you were ill. There was no such thing as a 'choice'
and fussy eaters just did without.

The Corn Exchange was also used as a cinema or 'the Pictures' and on Saturday nights adults and children queued on
the steps clutching coins and rushed in to get a 'good' seat.
Good behaviour was demanded even in moments of leisure
and if anyone dared even whisper to a friend during the film
they would find the light from the usher's torch dazzling their
eyes, and an angry 'Quiet!' would cause the culprit to sink
lower into jaggy upholstery. However, at the end of the film,
cheering was allowed, as was making a thunderous sound with
feet beating on the wooden floorboards. The 'back' door was
opened and a river of children rushed headlong down the stone

steps and made a beeline to the nearby 'chippy' to buy a bag of chips copiously anointed with salt and vinegar.

Opposite the Corn Exchange stood the marvellous Corner Shop with its magical 'penny counter'. We children would spend many anxious minutes deciding how to use our pocket money in the best way. The choices were considerable as many and varied were the sweets on display. Penny caramels, rhubarb rock, liquorice sticks resembling twigs, penny caramels, multicoloured spangles, sherbet, cheap unwrapped chocolate and a whole array of jewel-like sweets in glass jars all presented the young consumer with difficult decisions. After much consideration, it was usually the long-lasting, jaw-breaking gobstoppers that won the day. These amazing spheres, causing the consumer's cheek to bulge alarmingly would last for hours, changing colour as they diminished in size. They were often removed for inspection to identify each new shade. 'Lucky Bags' were indeed lucky as, inside the sweet, cocoa-covered 'potato' lay a small plastic toy. One nibbled carefully in order to keep the wee figure intact.

Near the Corner Shop stood Boa, the mecca of all ironmongers, whose shelves were laden with nails, brushes, wooden pegs, tools, paint, mousetraps, scrubbing brushes, mops, sugar soap, floor cloths, kindling for fires, paraffin, metal polish, candles, seeds, washing lines, dog collars, matches and much more. The shop had a specific smell unique to all ironmongers – a kind of sawdusty, turpentine aroma.

Every shop had its own distinctive smell and the pervasive aroma from the grocer's shop beside the burn at the foot of the High Street could be recognised yards away. Coffee and cheese were the two most dominant mouthwatering scents that enticed the prospective customer into Robert's domain. Robert always wore a grey dust coat. He was tall, thin and perpetually on the move round his emporium of exotic goods. To a child, unappreciative of home-made nourishing broths, his displays of tinned soups with mysterious names such as 'Asparagus', 'French Onion' and 'Mulligatawny' were unattainable gastronomic treats. Apples, oranges and bananas paled into insignificance as one studied the alluring pictures on the tins of rosy guavas, creamy lychees and golden mangos.

The vegetable and fruit displays only had the best of local produce and, in summer, Clyde Valley tomatoes with their distinctive aroma would lie side by side with fresh lettuce, syboes and cucumber. Robert sold wines and spirits and the local 'gentry' would order their purchases to be delivered to their various country seats near the town. Crates of whisky, hams, Patum Peperium, claret, cheeses, dark chocolate and coffee would travel in the shop van through the country lanes.

Robert had been christened 'the Thank-you Man' by an observant child due to his grateful demeanour when attending to a customer. A conversation might ensue as follows:

Customer:	'A pound of butter and a dozen eggs, please, Robert.'
Robert:	'Certainly. Thank you. Anything else?'
Customer:	'That will be all today.'
Robert:	'Thank you. Thank you.'
Customer:	'Goodbye.'
Robert:	'Thank you. Goodbye. Thank you.'

He had had the same approach with all his customers and was polite and helpful regardless of how much you were able to spend.

Beside Robert's was Nancy's small wool shop with floor-to-ceiling shelves stacked with all types and colours of wool. As women knitted many of the family garments, wool was an important item on the shopping list. Just as Mrs McGuffie could locate any article in her shop, Nancy knew exactly where to find any kind of wool. She would also keep her customer's desired brand and issue it when it was required. In that way, no one need buy a superfluous ball. Sheena's was another wool shop situated in the middle of town. It also had walls that seemed to be made of packets of wool. These often spilled over onto the floor causing prospective customers to push their way to the counter.

Across the main road from Nancy's, and near the burn, was the fishmonger whose window displays and fishy smells gave a seasidy feel to this part of town. Its windows cascaded with falls of ice-cold water through which could be seen creatures of the deep lying on their white-tiled resting place beside small lobster pots and shells. Crabs, lobsters, flounder, whiting, haddock, lemon sole and cod looked as fresh as if they had been caught that morning from the burn. The owner of the shop and his two assistants always had red noses and hands and, indeed, on entering from the street outside, it felt like stepping into a cool pool in summer, and a fridge in winter.

Many other small shops added character to the wide, tree-lined High Street. The doorway of the ironmongers, owned by the poet Gilbert Rae, was decorated with zinc buckets and wooden brushes. If sent on an errand to Bell the baker, it was impossible not to nibble at the newly baked warm bread as it was carried home loosely wrapped in white tissue paper. Paul the fishmonger also sold fruit and vegetables and his window displays featured eye-catching colourful patterns formed by whatever fresh produce was in season.

Delicious ice cream from the Townhead Café was enjoyed by everyone and visitors to the town would stroll round the shops eating a cone, wafer or the more expensive coconut sprinkled 'oysters'. As we enjoyed a lemonade at a small marble table in Caffola's Café we were often puzzled at the source of the mysterious aroma emanating from the kitchen. Future experiences would enlighten us to the fact that this had been garlic, used in the preparation of the Caffola family's meals.

We are fortunate if, in our towns, we still have our own distinctive shops providing individuality and character in an increasingly uniform world. Some of us are also fortunate to have colourful memories of the shopping experiences of our childhood. Perhaps the on-line customers of the future will remember shopping malls and hypermarkets with fondness and sigh for the metal trolleys and bar codes of their youth.

Whuppity Scoorie

T. Henry Shanks

The year was 1939. Not that dates meant a lot to an eight-year-old schoolboy. More importantly to a Lanark schoolboy it was '1st March – Whuppity Scoorie'. We had spent two hours in the classroom with our teacher, Miss Bruce, making the traditional newspaper balls and tying them securely to the long strings. We could not face the shame of them flying off or unwinding as we whirled them round our heads in the race around the kirk.

We had been trying on gasmasks at school for the first time. I hoped that the war would not come too soon. I was getting worried. I would be nine years old in October. If war came too early, I might not qualify for an adult-type gasmask. I had heard our neighbour Mrs Millar confide to my mother that, 'It'll no be lang noo.' This neighbourly blether on the doorstep was a big concession on the part of my mother, who used to be a lady's personal maid. Such informality was a sign of the serious nature of the times.

Our tea was finished early and my brother and I were getting ready for the 'big event'. We would not be waiting as usual for our Dad to come home from work this evening. My usual ride on the crossbar of his heavy Raleigh bike would have to wait until tomorrow. I could hear my mother's voice rising a bit, 'Hurry up you two, you'll miss Whuppity Scoorie this year, if it's still on with all this war business.' She was laughing as she shouted. She knew we wouldn't, couldn't. I knew at eight years of age that it was not likely to be cancelled. Certain things were aye done and Whuppity Scoorie (as well as Lanimers in June) was one of them. Anyway, I had seen the toon cooncil workmen hammering away at the stand at the Cross as I passed on my way home from school.

To my brother, Bill, my mother said, 'Now mind if it gets too rowdy, no running round the kirk. And keep hold of your wee brother's hand. And here don't forget your gloves.' It only took two minutes for us to skite down the cobbles of the Wide Close. They were polished like mirrors by the huge hooves of the Clydesdale. We were lucky we didn't have to wear tackety boots like some of our pals. There was no time this evening to stop at the door of the smiddy. Usually on our way to school, we stopped there, especially on cold winter mornings. Shalpit laddies, we lurked in the open doorway, lured by the red-hot glow of the furnace, the smell of the burning hooves with the din of stamping horses mingling with the driver's harsh shouts. We would watch until we were nearly late for school. The mighty Clydesdale leg would be tucked under the equally mighty muscular arm of the blacksmith as he set and hammered the iron shoe into the burning hoof. I often wondered if this was what Hell was like. I didn't fancy it too much.

No time for such thoughts tonight. We were too early at the Cross of course, because the proceedings could not start until the clock in the steeple had struck six times and the ancient wee bell had begun its first ring of the spring. That was what it meant to us. Spring did not start until the wee bell began its yearly duty. After our run round the kirk, waving paper balls around our heads, there was also, of course, the wild scrammle for pennies which the provost and the bailies produced from the deep pockets of their red robes. No problems about health and safety then. These dignitaries just chucked the money over our heads. Too bad if any of us were struck, I thought, as we wrestled over the copper coins. This must be what war feels like. At least we learned at an early age to keep our heads down. It could get vicious if some of the bigger boys had put stones in the centre of the paper balls and used them to clear the crowd.

When I thought about the war, I supposed that it would be a bit like the cowboy films we saw on the matinees at 'the Pictures' – except for the tanks and planes of course. Lots of explosions and shootings, but no blood. We knew from the Movietone News who to cheer – the Prime Minister of course, Neville Chamberlain, then Churchill. We knew to boo loudly the Nasties or Nazis and in particular, the chief baddie, Hitler.

Came June that year in the middle of a glorious hot summer, the citizens of the Royal Burgh of Lanark held the annual Lanimer celebrations – traditionally on a Thursday occurring between the sixth and twelfth days of June. With some of the soldiers being called up, there was much shaking of grey heads. Some said it would be the last one. I knew better. There were some magnificently decorated pageants and tableaux. Our Cub Scouts, in a continuing effort of austerity for the impending war, put in its usual entry of a handful of boys sitting on the back of a turf-layered old coal lorry. We were obviously cowboys as we wore our Cub neckerchiefs back to front, with borrowed Scout hats tilted to the back of our heads. One talented boy even had a guitar. We were not in the prize list.

We did not discuss the Munich Treaty. We knew vaguely

that a country called Poland might be invaded. Lanark, of course, was safe. We had the statue of William Wallace glowering up the High Street, sword at the ready.

Then, early in September, after the long hot summer, it happened. On 3 September at 11.15 am, we were in the garden – not at school. Through the open door and windows of the scullery the clipped, slightly metallic voice made the long-awaited announcement '... no such undertaking given ... this country is now at war with Germany.'

My mother came outside and said quietly to my brother, 'It's war again.' She did not sound anxious but she knew about war. She had three young sons who were likely to be much older before the war would be over. It was not long before the first wail of the air raid siren sounded – soon to be a familiar sound.

Held Up to the Light

Janis Mackay

> *'To dwell you must be content to listen.'*
> Jonathan Bate, *Song of the Earth*

I remember wearing white tap-dancing shoes, walking along a street in Edinburgh with my head down, staring at their scalloped front, their linen bow, their hard white material, their rounded toe, listening to their snap, snap, snap. And all there was in that moment was those adored white tap-dancing shoes. Now, looking back to those tap-dancing classes with Madame Ada in Regent's Terrace, I remember only queuing in line for fairy cakes and lemonade and being told to stand up straight, but it's the memory of wonder, staring down at my white dancing shoes on a city street that remains.

Where place is a sense of wonder.

That place where the child lives.

Back then, Saturdays were the 'warushhh warushhh' of the Bex Bisell carpet-sweeper, the whack of cane against rugs hung over the washing line, go-karts round the block, the smell of Mr Sheen and changing pink nylon sheets. Saturday dinner was 'just soup and pudding' then we'd take the 42 up town to Patrick Thompson's, Binns, Lawsons, Timber, Goldbergs,

C & A's, Jenners. Was it in a dark-brown and musty Jenners that prim ladies in fawn cardigans put rolled-up pieces of paper into a magic tube where they were then whisked with a whoosh magically across the shop?

By age 12 or 13, Saturday afternoon was torches flashed in our faces by tough-looking 16 or 17-year-old girls in the George Picture House, Portobello, and being told 'Oot!' because one of us had giggled. We would all troop out, needing to keep the gang intact, and drift down to the shows where hungry-looking boys would press their hard bodies against Crompton's Cake Walk for a fistful of tipped coppers. Rich raspy 'this is your lucky day' voices declared through megaphones that 'two fat ladies were 88, all the threes were 33 and six and nine made 69.' It was a kind of poetry. Poetry with a hard, cheap, trinkety edge that held women in thrall.

I'd walk home with a goldfish in a plastic bag that might live for a day or two.

I can still see them, those little orange fish in three clear inches of water, clutched in a plastic bag and held up to the light of fruit machines and sea, and can smell still the seaweed and sewage tang of Seafield.

The fish is not dead.

After the shows and a bottle of Sun Kool Cola, it was home to the drone of the results, hypnotic and belonging to Saturdays, like pink newspapers, Spot the Ball and shouting men. Places I didn't know would take on a familiarity through the repeated sound of their names: 'Queen of the South 2 St Mirren 3, Kilmarnock 4 Motherwell 2, Partick Thistle 1 Airdrie 1, Scottish League division three, Dunfermline 3 Arbroath 2.' And as long as his voice continued there was order in the world … rhythm, like the poetry of places even more mysterious: North of Sirra South of Sirra German Bite Dogger Fastnet Lund Irish Sea.

A stick of rhubarb in a bowl of sugar, a tin bath in front of a coal fire, Dixon of Dock Green, Shirley Bassey, Liberace ... and we would sit there exercising our jaws on Curly Wurlys, cola bottles, traffic lights, black jacks, fruit salads, midget gems, flying saucers ...

Sunday had a wider, whiter breath. My face pressed against the window of the Standard Super Ten, later the Ford Capri, where landmarks etched their shapes and names to me, so that now, years later, I can still see things the way they were. Sam Burns' junkyard before he built himself a fancy house, the open-air swimming pool at Port Seton and the sound of rain falling into the warm water, lit as it fell by the green and red floodlights around the pool. And over the wall, the wild sound of the dark and crashing sea. That it was the Firth of Forth was just another way of saying the sea. To the child I was, this sea was enough, from Portobello to Joppa, along to Longniddry Bents, Aberlady, Gullane, Yellowcraigs, Direlton, North Berwick, Dunbar. The words rolled out like the winding road itself.

On those Sunday trips, 'going out in the car', we would have time, heading east, to go through our repertoire of the 'Sound of Music', 'Coming Round the Mountain' and the 'Quartermaster's Stores'. I would have no idea what a quartermaster was but loved the way the tune would rise and fall, belting out from the back of the car. 'I've left my specs in the double you sea.'

The sand dunes at Gullane sloped down from tufted corn-coloured marran grass to stretches of golden sand. I'd suck sharp sandthorn berries and queue for a Mr Whippy slider, oyster or 99. From the beach you could look back and see Edinburgh and always there was the shape of Arthur's Seat, unless there was a haar. We loved the word and said it as though the vowel went on forever.

Those Sunday beach trips felt like a holiday, family, open place, wild place. Old people would doze on beach chairs set up next to their cars, Austin Maxis or Allegros. Or they would be nibbling neat sandwiches from Tupperware then sipping steaming tea from brown plastic flasks and gazing out to sea and over to Fife. Then, less tame, sprawled down on the beach, the extended families. They would have moved in with striped windbreakers and their place already claimed and marked out for rounders. There would be a few blow-up lilos and rubber rings, maybe even a blow-up crocodile and tartan rugs sprawled across the sand spread with raffia baskets, newspapers, picnic cool bags, buckets, spades, plastic plates and Ambre Solaire suntan oil. And women with bright blowy blouses unbuttoned to reveal large white cross-your-heart bras with freckled flesh rolling over the straps. Teenagers with radios up to their ears, bright plastic beach balls, loud calling voices and children in towelling swimsuits crying, getting a sweetie, then laughing and running off.

On the way back, sand in socks, we would stop at S. Luca in Musselburgh for tea. I thought it was St Luca. There always seemed to be a queue and we would wait, it was part of it, enjoying the expectation. I remember a treat, getting a knickerbocker glory, full of tinned fruit and vanilla, chocolate *and* strawberry ice cream. It came in a fancy fluted glass with a slim long-handled spoon and was a kind of heaven. I don't know though what was the richer, the sweet ice cream in my mouth or the evocative place names of the East Lothian coast and how even now they taste of childhood, free spaces, summer and Sundays.

After St Luca and me wondering if everyone in Musselburgh was really honest, we'd be welcomed home at the foot of Milton Road by a wooden sign saying 'Edinburgh – The Festival City'.

I liked to come from a place that defined itself by the word 'Festival'. It suggested parties, celebrations and wonder. And Edinburgh sounded like Eden (I went to Sunday school) and so to grow up, living in the Garden of Eden having celebrations of wonder, had a positive, upbeat purity about it.

I remember the Festival as being a coloured cavalcade of lorries dressed up and going along Princes Street very slowly, tooting horns, and on them, these 'floats', people half-naked in grass skirts or bright clothes, would wave, sing, dance and play trumpets and guitars. We families would line Princes Street cheering and waving and singing along. Then there were the fire-eaters and street musicians down the Royal Mile and people who spoke foreign languages taking photographs of each other, making sure the Castle was in the background. These different voices awoke a wider world in me and later I would learn them, follow their mystique. Apart from these exotic voices and tall blond people, the word 'tourist' in Edinburgh, to the child that I was, was synonymous with rich Americans in bright yellow tartan trousers, size extra large.

Each August my aunt and uncle would take me to see the Oxford Revue where we would laugh and clap, and laugh and clap and then we had done the Festival.

Later on, I went away.

Now, I have come back.

It is sunny in August in the city so I am out, under *Toona sinensis* who is under *Larix xeurolepsis* who is under bright blue sky and sun. Toona has bent off east to make space for her bright green foliage, her stretching limbs. She is a salad bowl tossed with crow squawk croutons. And here is a dancer with his woody legs arabesquing the Botanical air, his daft head in the soil. Now I am hiding under *Juniperus rigida* and I can tell you her trunk is sinewy and sexy. Under here, her hair is a copper autumn although it's still August, and hangs down like the hop bunches in Kent pubs. When the soft wind lifts, her branches as one, tilt like a ship and I am a passenger aboard a tree. Her trunk anchors well, splayed out like mossed vulnerable vaginas as she enters the earth.

In Inverleith House, Iain Hamilton Findlay has made sentences that paper the white quiet walls. 'The sound of bees,' he writes, 'is a weather ... that of wood pigeons too.' Here today, in late August, in the Botanic Gardens, in Edinburgh, the weather is wind in grand trees, bushes and rushes; is the soft percussion of toddlers' feet, small and flat on the stone slabs by the café; is couples who are comfortable with each other, pressing their faces close, not talking, eating sultana scones.

And I let in the wind, the trees, the stone, the green spaces. I let in the children, the mothers, the sentences, the Latin names. I let in Tim Stead. My shoulder blades press against the wooded throne he made for the Pope.

I sit on a throne in Edinburgh and let in memory and the blessed dead.

The skyline from here is well kent. Through parted pine branches I see Calton Hill and what looks like one huge breast (the Observatory), the Nelson Monument, Hellenic Folly and beyond these, Arthur's Seat.

Later I climb all 143 steps of that monument and take in the sweep of the place. Over to Fife and the mountains beyond, the soft rolling backcloth of the Pentland Hills, on Calton Hill a circle of friends are sharing a baguette, figures are dark shapes in Princes Street in the shadow of the sloping late afternoon sun, the Parliament building looks organic, it bends, breathes, the Palace behind stands solemn and grand in a square, an alarm is going off by St Leonards, the sound of frantic sirens at the top of Leith Walk, there is a bus going along Ferry Road, and figures moving on Salisbury Crags, the still calm of the Firth of Forth curving round to stretches of beach and the coastal place names I could chant, my old school, and blots on this view like the Scottish offices behind the St James Centre, like my old school ... the trees sloping away from Calton Hill to London Road are already tinged with autumn, office workers are leaving St Andrew's House, the green man must be on at Waterloo Place, everyone is crossing the road, there is the clock tower of St Stephen Street, the oasis of Botanics, rows of glass over Waverley Station, and the Castle, the great and craggy Castle, housing the Honours and oor ancient stane, turn east to islands in the estuary, a plane coming in over the Forth, the road and rail bridges, like pulled sleeves stretched north over still water, look west to a lazy Lion Rampant, dark spires rising at the West End, and everywhere domes, spires, statues and weathervanes of the city and down to a girl reading in the grass below.

I have been out on the Diaspora and long for nests, shells, crofts, songs.

I have come home, to be caught up in the buzz of Fringe and Festival – welcome to Edinburgh, the Festival City. Wonderful bustle but, just for now, more full of world than the small part I reach for.

England has been like an aunt and good to me, as I have been good to her. We have brought much to each other. But Scotland, that much closer relation, like an elusive lover, is proving hard to find.

I take myself off to the Gallery of Modern Art. Sit on a green ridge of the Landform and watch the kidney shape of shallow water and curves of tamed grass.

I watch a pregnant woman, who well knows her friend's camera is following her, and knows the microphone clipped to her shirt is recording her. I watch her rip a daisy, chanting as she poses and scatters its tiny white petals to the gentle wind: 'he loves me, he loves me not.'

And just right now, I'm about sick of it. Fringed out. After eight years south I return to Scotland and in every hip café, Fringe box office and with every flyer shoved into my hand, it is Covent Garden, Camden Lock.

Days I'd reach for Scots voices in the tame Sussex air as though they were homing pigeons.

And I realise sense of place and homecoming is a return to the sound of the place, the voices, the place names, the way things are said.

It's not only the well-kent skylines, the rumble of maroon buses over cobbled streets, the one o'clock gun, tenements, closes, cafes, Irn Bru, ragwort, rosebay willowherb, rowan, birch, the curlew, the way the hills break open and rise or great feathery Saltires in the northern sky ... but voices, grounded, lilting, deep, rolling ... the first songs and sounds, the susurrus – the way things are said.

A busload of teenagers arrives. They scatter themselves around the Landform and around me, writing. I count 42 of them. They are probably in the 5th or 6th year at school. They're from Glasgow: big lads with football tops and baggy jeans, girls with blond streaks, tummies, hipster belts and kohl-rimmed eyes. They get out their sketchpads and I watch them. They are quick to get down to it. They are intent, look up, around, look down, they concentrate, they let the place absorb them, they draw.

And I am drinking their voices, their sense of gratitude and wonder and the way they attend to the place. They, and me, and the pregnant woman and her friend and Francis Bacon and David Hockney and Henri Cartier-Bresson and everyone here – we are the place.

A big lad looks up from his drawing and says to his pal, 'It's a beautiful day for sketching.' Then his friend looks up from his sketching and replies, 'Aye, it is a beautiful day.'

And I have blown open like Miranda, wearing those white tap-dancing shoes again, saying 'Brave new world, that has such people in it.'

I want to hug them. Turn round and say, 'So it is.'

But I say nothing.

They sketch.

I write.

It is.

Farm Boy

Bill MacKenzie

School was always hard. In the spring, with the sounds of tractors teasing us from the fields and swallows skimming mockingly past the classroom windows, it was doubly so.

Bird nesting was our passion. The nests and eggs were never disturbed but all were methodically counted. The exceptions were the seagulls' nests on Invercharron Hill and on the stones beside the river. These nests were so glaringly easy to find that we did not add them to our tally. Only from the gulls did we take eggs. We carried them home by the dozen in knotted hankies. There, dubious mothers fried them or used them for baking though the redness of the yolks gave the scones an unusual hue and they were eaten in private like a sin.

And then the turnips were through. We sharpened our hoes and entered the hoeing match. We kids had three short sections of drill each. We painstakingly smoothed the soil and laid each turnip smartly at right angles to the razor sharp drill. There was an endless prize list. As well as the first, second and third in every age and sex section, there were prizes for: the first finished, the last finished, the youngest, the oldest, most recently married, most recent father (or mother), the furthest travelled, best local, best from Caithness, best from Sutherland,

best from Ross-shire, best from Kincardine, best from Creich.
And I have forgotten a few. One had to be very unremarkable
and very unlucky to escape winning a prize for something.

I did not need to worry about razor edges and such finer
points when I joined the regular squad in the field. The group
varied from day to day. Permanently in number one position
was Duncan's son. Then came the full-time farm workers,
including Geordie the shepherd if he couldn't find a good
enough excuse to be elsewhere. Then came the crofters, mostly
old men who worked for a couple of days in return for favours
– one of which was sexual, for their cow would be brought to
the Invercharron bull. And last in line came me.

At the end of each long drill there was a pause while pipes
were filled and fags rolled and they waited for me to finish.
As soon as I arrived they were ready to start again and the
injustice of that, which meant that I got no break between
drills, has stayed with me to this day. But there were a couple
of longer breaks when flasks were produced. On a few days of
exceptional heat, or just because he fancied a blether, Duncan
would arrive with bottles of beer. I was allowed one – warm
and frothy like used bath water – which I drank with pride.

And there was always the talk. Some of the older men had
been in the First War and we got yarns about foreign places
and foreign people. Occasionally they would forget that they
were being tailed by a kid with big, flappy ears and discuss more
risqué subjects. Old Watt was good for the more exotic tales
of far-flung women. But Usdean was a Wee Free and didn't
like that sort of talk and would snort and spit and eventually
raise my presence as an excuse for censorship (I used to try to
be present when he brought his cow to the bull. You could tell
he didn't like me being there. He didn't like being there himself.) Geordie did not approve of some of Watt's stories either.

Geordie had been in the army too but had obviously missed out on a lot and he cast doubt on Watt's accounts. Watt was not pleased.

To the casual observer, it would appear that the local sheep-dog trials were as fair a test as could be devised for man and dog. The set up of the gates, the position of the pen and the award of points was the same for everyone. But there were variables and in charge of variables was Watt. At the bottom end of the field, far from the scrutiny of competitors and audience, there was a large corral of sheep which it was Watt's responsibility to release in batches of five for each handler. The sheep were locals from Invercharron and some were brought in from Croick to make up the numbers.

Experts in local geography will testify that it is difficult to find a flatter piece of land than Invercharron, wedged as it is between the Kyle and the Carron. They will be hard pressed to name a hillier farm than Croick. The Invercharron sheep lived on the lushest grass, their poor relations from Croick nibbled the odd grass blade they could find among the heather. The top speed of the fat Invercharron ewes was a sedate trot while the lanky Croick toughs could jump and run like the deer with whom they competed for grazing.

The shepherd who Watt issued with five Invercharron ewes only had himself or his dog to blame if the flock ambled past a gate instead of through it. By the time they reached the pen they would be so breathless that they would gladly enter in the belief that they might there have a rest.

The handler who was given Croick sheep had a more daunting task. The main problem was that the sheep could outrun all but the swiftest dog. When presented with the novelty of a flat surface, their main aim seemed to be to head for the surrounding hills – and they did not break their stride when they came upon a wimpish field fence, they were used to deer fences. It was not unusual for such a group of hooligans to avoid all obstacles and demoralise the dog and humiliate the handler.

When Geordie had cast doubt on some of Watt's tales at the hoeing, Watt just smiled and sucked his pipe and said, 'Maybe, maybe!' Geordie had probably forgotten the incident before the end of the day. Watt had not. He bided his time and now his time had come.

Geordie strolled confidently to the post which marked the handler's position and his sleek collie came so close in his wake that his nose might have been glued to Geordie's boot. Five Invercharron sheep for Geordie? His lifelong pal Watt would surely oblige. But Watt bore a grudge. So five Croick stags, then? That would indeed be a crushing riposte for a past slight. But Watt could do better than that.

Sheep from the same flock will generally stick together in a tight group. Different flocks offer no such allegiance. So when, through his telescope, Watt spied Geordie's walk to the post, he had his assistants release three Croick sheep and two Invercharron ones.

When the groups were released at the bottom of the field, they normally got their heads down for a bit of a snack while, unseen, the dog made a wide sweep to approach them from behind and gently chivvy them towards, and then through, the various obstacles. That was the usual and clearly the Invercharron ewes knew what was expected of them and began peacefully to graze. The others looked around and then fled doing jumps which would not have disgraced a springbok. When they met a strange, surprised dog they smartly about-turned and fled towards the opposite horizon buffeting the peaceful grazers with the slipstream of their passing.

There were three options for Geordie. He could have called

his dog to heel and retired with grace. He could have had his dog guide the two peaceful participants through the course – he would gain no points but it would have saved face a bit. Or he could send his poor dog to try and retrieve the runaways and return them to the starting point to rejoin the two who showed no inclination to go anywhere.

Sadly for Geordie he chose the third option and we all knew he was on a loser. Geordie was a stubborn man. He was a loud man. And he had a short temper. Having set out on a course he stuck to it valiantly and as he sent his dog back and forth across the field chasing the three miscreants, he got louder and more and more heated.

There was a time limit for course completion but long before his time was up the whistle was blown – as Duncan afterwards quietly explained, 'To save the dog from exhaustion and Geordie from a heart attack.' At the end of the day Geordie won the prize for 'the Most Noise' so he was somewhat mollified, though he never spoke to Watt again.

The days after the trials might have been an anticlimax but there was all the activity of dismantling the course and taking down the tents to keep us going. And even when that was done there was one more pleasure we could screw out of it – on our knees we searched the trodden grass which marked the bar in the beer tent. Mostly we only got coppers with an occasional sixpence but we did (sadly only once) find half-a-crown.

A boy could always make himself useful in the harvest. Hay was the first main harvest. There were no balers so the hay was brought into the stackyard loose and as a result a residue lay still scattered across the field. It was the perfect job for a horse, a boy and a rake. We crossed and recrossed the field gathering the scattered leftovers. I sat on the iron seat high above the rake and twice on each crossing I leaned precariously out to pull the handle to lift the tines. The result when the job was done was to be two neat rows of hay which could be easily collected and gathered in. The horse needed little direction. She plodded from one side of the field to the other without much reference to the proud pipsqueak on the iron seat. Had she objected there was little I could do. She was a big beast, with powerful feathered legs and feet the size of dinner plates.

But in every Eden there is a serpent. In my and the mare's little bit of heaven there were the clegs. They swarmed round horse and boy. Boy could bash them when they bit but horse could not. So at every end-rig we paused and I clambered down from my perch and went round her squishing them. Her skin trembled where the clegs sucked. She was a greyish red colour which made her look old but she was young enough to have a spark of the devil in her and she was not above having a little tap dance and that was when I had to look lively to avoid the dinner plates. To add to her tendency towards skittishness the mare had one blind eye which resulted in a lot of head tossing – and her head was as hard as her hooves and was best avoided. She was perpetually anxious about what was happening on her blind side so as I squished the clegs on that side I had to keep up a monologue of assurance.

But the real harvest – the harvest we all thought about when we sang about 'All is safely gathered in' in the church – was the corn harvest. By my time there was no part for the mare to play in that job. The tractor pulled the binder and we followed behind bowing like worshippers stooking the sheaves. In that heaven, the devil for the stookers was in the thistles. For the men it was the knotter in the binder. There would be regular hold-ups when the followers realised that the sheaves which the binder was spitting out were not tied. The tractor would be yelled to a halt and the men would gather round the knotter to inspect and cajole. For the men it was a puzzle when the mechanism went wrong. For me it was a wonderment – which lasts still – that any machine could tie a knot so my puzzlement was when it went right.

If the weather was good the reaping went on into dusk and such days lay an impression of beauty on my mind which is still as fresh as it was 50 years ago. The binder sails turning, white and unhurried, in the gloom the pale gleam of the corn and above it all the moon – huge and low and orange, the kind of moon that causes a shiver of joyous wonder even in a callow loon.

Then it was winter. In the first grudging light it was back to the turnip field to throw some oats and hay to the sheep. The freezing wind penetrated to the bones and gnawed at the marrow. Too cold for snow but flurries of hail shrapnelled in on the wind and lay in little drifts on the frozen earth and stirred and twirled like venomous sand.

The sheep needed no calling to come to be fed. They were spread across the ridged field gnawing on frozen turnips which were ice-welded into the soil but when they heard the Fergie they began to run. By the time I reached the feeding troughs all but the lamest were milling around the tractor and trailer. I forked hay into the hakes and then jumped down and shouldered the bag of oats and nuts. As I walked along the line of feedboxes I poured an even ration along each trough. Not as easy as it sounds with anxious animals trying to push me aside and trip me up – no better manners than I expected from these evil possessors of the devil's eye. I pitied the sheep as the wind zipped hail, spitting and hissing. But they turned scornful eyes and I knew that they preferred this iron, hoof-tapping ground to the previous weeks of deep, heavy mud.

Then gloriously back to the steading and into the gloom.

Wind rattled the door and the corrugated iron roof but there in the byre it was warm with the body heat and gusting breath and sweet with the smell of hay and fresh dung. I clicked the switch, tickled by the novelty of electricity, and two dusty bulbs glowed, creating more shadow than light. Big horned heads turned in my direction and paused their chewing jaws for one beat – no more.

Down the rows of stalls I went, scraping the soiled straw and dung into the gutter. Shouldering aside obstinate rears, wary round the hind end of the red rogue kicker, the grape ringing on the concrete. Then brush and grape to clear the gutter and back and fore with fresh straw to renew bedding – an extra armful to the calves to allow for cosy nests. Hay, full of clover and some sharp thistles, smelling of a dusty summer, I piled into the hakes above the cows' heads; turnips, spilt in the finger-threatening cutter, a basket full in front of each beast causing a crescendo of crunching; checked the water and then stood back. The calves standing watchful on big-kneed legs suddenly pranced or danced or plunged beneath their mothers to assuage an amazingly sudden hunger.

Leith Central Station

Tim Bell

I'm a country boy, really. When I came visiting my brother in
Edinburgh in the late 1970s, I thought Leith Walk was a riot
of colour and fun. All those pubs, Asian shops, people getting
on and off buses. Then in 1980 we moved to Edinburgh, and
by a stroke of luck, the size of which I didn't realise at the time,
we got a family house in Leith. I set about becoming a Leither.
One thing puzzled me: an old man told me the heart of Leith
was at 'the Fit ay the Walk'. I went, looked, walked round,
but couldn't see or feel any heart. All I could see was a busy
city junction, the scruffy downtown end of a street of many
moods. There was a nice bit of pavement facing south, looking
up Leith Walk towards Edinburgh. Behind was a rather disa-
greeable shopping centre which led onto a charmless walkway
through some housing blocks. To the left was a curved façade
of something grander which had disappeared, and on top of
the curve, the street corner, was a clock which, rather pleas-
ingly, always told the right time. Under the clock was the entrance to the Job Centre, attracting a sort of listlessness. You
often find that. The pub set within the façade had obviously
seen better days. Right opposite the pub, across several lanes
of Leith Walk traffic, was an office of the Halifax Building

Society. Handy for us – they owned most of our house. But where was this heart of the community? We'll have to go back a bit.

The 20th century was probably the worst in Leith's history. For most of the millennium it had been the landing stage for capital and country, a working, seafaring town accustomed to the great comings and goings to do with that Castle up the hill, with connections far beyond the horizon. Mary, Queen of Scots, landed here in 1561. It must have been a nice day, as she said she was pleased to be in 'sunny Leith'. But in truth the new merchant city of Glasgow was better placed to take advantage of the Atlantic trade from the 16th century onwards, and from then Leith began to lose its prominence. Even so, as late as the 1770s it was seriously proposed that the capital should shift from the crowded and unhealthy Edinburgh High Street to a green-field site beside the sea. But from commanding the river mouth so perfectly proportioned for medieval shipping, it was steel and industrialisation that really did for Leith. For half a century up to the Great War the railways could have goods off the ships and rattling across Scotland within hours. But they tore up the railway lines, and introduced steel containers. No modern port can be boxed in by city streets. Most of the 20th century was spent in decline.

Of course, Leith fared no worse than many other places during the 1920s and 30s. Sure, there was a small revival during the Second World War: something like 65 per cent of the landing craft, pontoons and other hardware used during the Normandy landings were built at Henry Robb's shipyard, on the site where Ocean Terminal now stands. But the decline in shipping was inexorable, and during the 1950s, 60s, and 70s the decline accelerated, taking with it the associated maritime industries. Leith was losing not only good jobs; it was losing its sea-facing focus. To make matters worse, even land-based workplaces found themselves unable to resist government relocation grants. Edinburgh Crystal for one, who found themselves in Penicuik before you could raise a glass. The Department of Trade and Industry would have its way. And, employing the wisdom of the day, the council decanted much of the town-centre population to housing schemes, mainly to the west of Leith: Pilton, Pennywell, Muirhouse; though elsewhere also, for example Oxgangs.

It is difficult now to find any excuse for those vast badly planned and badly built schemes, under the ownership of the local authority which had the task of acting as landlord thrust upon it without any clear rationale or policy. Many families, including Mr and Mrs Welsh and their son Irvine, had left a town with its centuries-old structures, institutions and middle-class, for these places that were supposed to answer the needs of a single socioeconomic group. The open spaces quickly became unattractive and even unsafe with broken glass and dog shit. The planners had no intention of letting shops and pubs start a business where there was demand. That sort of thing was grouped around shopping centres. The one on Pennywell Road is typical: unattractive in appearance, unappealing to walk round and linger in, and the shopkeepers always struggle to make a living. The units were never designed for family businesses anyway – branches of chain shops are far more common. The banks are noticeable by their absence, seeing no market for themselves, leaving financial services in the hands of loan sharks. Thus is spontaneous and healthy economic life and social intercourse stifled and stilted. Inevitably a generation grew up with little knowledge of, or stake in, wider society. In his novel *Trainspotting*, Irvine Welsh later depicted the toilet in the bookie's in the shopping centre as a fantastically, grotesquely, foul place. The film of the novel dubbed it the 'worst toilet in Scotland'.

But, back to Leith town centre. The medieval Kirkgate (Church Street, in modern English) was for centuries the main artery of the town. By a few hundred yards it was away from the working area of the river mouth, the Shore. It was also away from the old working roads from Edinburgh. Easter Road came from Abbey Strand, the only place you could get a horse and cart off Edinburgh High Street and the Canongate, by the east of Calton Hill to the bottom of the Shore. Wester Road – now lost, but in the modern street pattern roughly following Calton Road, Broughton Street and Bonnington Road – came by the west of Calton Hill to the top of the Shore. The relatively new Leith Walk (a leftover from the Civil War), that mile-long broad boulevard that delivers traffic direct from Edinburgh, stops short of interfering with the older street. The Kirkgate was a string of small shops and offices with wynds between them. There was even a little theatre: The Gaiety. Known as 'the Channel', the Kirkgate was rough and ready, perhaps intimidating to the stranger, but lived in and loved, the place where Leith was at its most distinctive. By the 1960s it was certainly in need of a bit of sorting out and sensitive restoration. But in an act of civic vandalism it was demolished in 1964, the only buildings to survive being the venerable Trinity House, a monument to former prosperity and seafaring traditions, and the kirk. Once again the shops and various community functions were bundled together into another of those bleak shopping centres at the top, and the northern end was converted to a walkway that you can see again anywhere from south London to Chicago. After all the disinvestments and fragmentation throughout Leith, truly the heart of the town was torn out. And just opposite the top of the Kirkgate, at the Fit ay the Walk, was Leith Central Station.

A latecomer in railway history, Leith Central Station was opened in 1903. The council insisted on a clock tower over the entrance to the platforms on the corner of Leith Walk and Duke Street – a nice touch, that. Just to the south of the platforms they had an enormous multi-ridged roof over the sidings yard – like the Waverley station roof you see from North Bridge – which was supported by the boundary wall and various props within. The station was intended to catch the commuter market to Edinburgh. Optimistic, you might say, but at the time Leith and Edinburgh, which were separate municipalities, operated different tram systems. Halfway up the Walk, right outside the Boundary Bar at Pilrig, the systems met. 'If you want to go to Edinburgh, get a tram to Pilrig and walk,' they said. The trains did well enough until they sorted out 'the Pilrig Muddle', and then the commuter market died away. But not the station. An everyday, boring commuter station it wasn't. This was Leith's access to the outside world, the terminus for epic journeys. The company laid on football specials, pulling crowds to and from the Hibs matches across Scotland, who would walk the half-mile up Easter Road to the stadium. The Central Bar – the station buffet – was designed and furnished in the same vein as the Café Royal in Edinburgh. Illustrations of possible destinations were painted on the tiles: sailing at the seaside, highland scenes, golf in East Lothian. You could have a drink there and walk straight onto the platform. Comings and goings, families and football, vision and dreams, energy and excitement: all this could be found at the Fit ay the Walk, at Leith Central Station. But without a commuter market it didn't last long enough to be closed by Dr Beeching in the 1960s. The last train pulled out of Leith Central Station in 1953. In a sure sign of a slack economy, the entire edifice was left standing empty for some 30 years.

I don't remember the old sidings under the shed roof at all.

I suppose it was closed off and we weren't encouraged to look there. But a friend who lived right beside the site tells me she worried about the bairns playing on the roof, how dangerous it was, how undesirable characters used to get in there, and what they got up to. At the time of writing, the site of the old platforms is occupied by a Scotmid supermarket and the misconceived and badly built Leith Waterworld. I'm glad they don't call it a swimming pool, because you can't get a straight swim, it's all waves, chutes, and bubbles. The latest word is that it's going to be demolished after less than 20 years of life. The old sidings are a car park. Apart from the façade on Leith Walk and Duke Street all that remains of Leith Central Station is the shape of the premises and the strong wall that used to support the roof on the south side. Notice of the demolition of the station had been given when Irvine Welsh works his metaphor that summarises and gives its name to his novel *Trainspotting*. Mark Renton, from Leith, is coming home from London for Christmas. He walks out of Waverley Station onto Calton Road, under the Waterloo Arch, onto Leith Street, past the Playhouse, and down Leith Walk. He meets a childhood friend, Frank Begbie, now a violent, brutal, cynical man, at Tommy Younger's, then a very traditional pub subsequently renamed The Walk Inn and now known as Jayne's Bar and Bistro:

The pair ay us then leave the pub thegither and head doon the Walk. Ah jist want tae git ma heid doon at ma Ma's, but The Beggar insists ah come back tae his bit fir a bevvy. We go for a pish in the auld Central Station at the Fit ay the Walk, now a barren, desolate hangar, soon tae be demolished and be replaced by a supermarket and a swimming centre. Somehow that makes us sad, even though ah wis eywis too young to mind ay trains ever being there.

– Some size ay a station this wis. Git a train tae anywhair fae

*here at one time, or so they sais, ah sais, watching ma steaming
pish splash oantae the cauld stane.*

*– If it still hud fuckin trains, ah'd be oan one oot ay this fuckin
dive, Begbie said. It wis uncharacteristic for him tae talk aboot
Leith in that way. He tended to romanticise the place.*

*An auld drunkard, whom Begbie had been looking at, lurched up
tae us, wine boatil in his hand. Loads ay them used this place tae
bevvy and crash in.*

*– What yis up tae, lads? Trainspotting, eh? He sais, laughing
uncontrollably at his ain fucking wit.*

*–Aye, that's right, Begbie sais. Then under his breath:–fucking
auld cunt.*

*– Ah well, ah'll leave yis tae it. Keep up the trainspotting,
mind!*

*He staggered oaf, his rasping drunkard's cackles filling the desolate
barn.*

Irvine Welsh, *Trainspotting*

Come and stand with me, on a nice day in Sunny Leith, where
the cars turn at the end of the long car park, Scotmid to our
left, Leith Waterworld just beyond it, and with our backs to
the lovely old stone wall that used to keep up the roof over the
sidings. In the fiction it is the end of the year. For Renton and
Begbie, abusers of drugs and alcohol, it is a triumph to get to
the end of a year. Their friend Lesley's wee baby Dawn has
died. They have just been to Matty's funeral. Tommy is far
gone with AIDS. And the year ahead does not beckon with
the exciting invitation that you and I look forward to. In their
chaotic lifestyles, these young men have made no plans. If they
are still here this time next year, that will be another triumph.
The end of the year brings intimations of mortality to mind.
And they are standing at the end of the line. The wall behind

us is the end of the line. They are in a dirty, dangerous, derelict place that is due for demolition and oblivion. And they are pissing in it. The metaphor is inescapable. It could hardly be bleaker. And, to add to the pain, a ghostly figure comes out of the shadows and makes the ridiculous, futile suggestion that they are trainspotting, three and a half decades after the last train left. Who is this ghost? The ghost of a generation of unemployed Leith men? The ghost of a man who has lost his life to alcohol? And what ghost train is he looking for? The glorious happy days of Leith community, so closely focused on Leith Central Station? Those days are gone, but he has found nothing better to look for and wait for.

This episode, with its metaphor, sums up the themes of the book to this point. There has been no great story, rather a series of loosely connected episodes mainly based on the four main characters (though others come from nowhere and go without trace), mainly placed in Leith and Edinburgh, and mainly centred on the dark themes of drugs and alcohol (though it's not without humour). If you have only seen the film *Trainspotting* you have no idea why it is so called. Nothing in the content suggests its title. But it's hard to make the metaphor work for you even from the pages of the book unless you know the place and its history and meaning.

The end of the book seems to be saying something else about Leith and its people: all four main characters, Renton, Begbie, Sick Boy and Spud, end up in London, strangers, losers, out of their depth and at odds with each other. There's no talk of coming back. In reality lots of people left Leith for a better life elsewhere.

By the mid-to-late 1990s the results of public money spent on infrastructure in Leith, combined with the drive of the now privatised docks, were beginning to show. The first large success for the policy of attracting investment came from the government itself: the low sheds on the south side of the unused Victoria Dock were removed to make way for the Scottish Office (now the Scottish Executive, and known within the Civil Service as Victoria Quay), in an instant bringing 1,500 sustainable good quality jobs to Leith. A bus service ran to and from Fife for the commuters. The Bank of Scotland and Forth Ports invested in Ocean Terminal to replace Henry Robb's shipyard, and Donald Dewar worked a minor miracle in inducing the former Royal Yacht *Britannia* (one of Scotland's top tourist attractions) to tie up alongside. Once again Leith was seriously considered as a site for a capital function, the new Scottish Parliament, but they chose Holyrood instead. Town bus routes were diverted and invented, beating a path to Leith docks for the money-spending visitor and tourist.

Trainspotting's sequel, *Porno*, catches up with the same characters ten years later, the very time of all this change. Sick Boy has been in London for ten years, and is impressed. He has acquired what in reality is the Port o' Leith pub on Constitution Street, and here he reviews his prospects:

The place is a potential gold mine, just waiting for a makeover job. You can feel the gentrification creeping up from the Shore and forcing house prices up and I can hear the tills ringing as I give the Port Sunshine a tart-up from Jakey Central to New Leith café society … Leith is on the up. It'll be on the Tube line before Hackney. I'm walking further down into the new Leith: the Royal Yacht Britannia, the Scottish Office, renovated docks, wine bars, restaurants, yuppie pads. This is the future, and it's only two blocks away. The next year, the year after, maybe, just one block away. Then bingo!

Irvine Welsh, *Porno*

But it is to Leith Central Station that Welsh returns for the climax of *Porno*. At the end of a long and involved plot Begbie, sitting in the Central Bar, gets a call from Sick Boy to tell him Renton, whom he fully intends to murder, is in town. He goes outside to get a better signal on his mobile, and there he is! Renton is taking money from the ATM at the Halifax opposite. Spud comes across the scene a few minutes later. It's the first time they are brought together since the end of *Trainspotting*, with the arch-manipulator Sick Boy present on his mobile. There in the shadow of Leith Central Station, just off the top of the Kirkgate, at the Fit ay the Walk, they collide.

What is so important about Leith Central Station to Welsh that he puts it at the heart of both these books? Is he nodding to that man who told me where to find the heart of Leith?

Libraries of Love and Passion

Donald Smith

Edinburgh is a bookish city. If the New Town represents classically ordered and catalogued shelves, then the Old is a profusion of volumes piled higgledy-piggledy ready to hand for the reader sunk in an armchair or in the snug of a Cowgate bar.

There are of course libraries aplenty, each with their devoted readers and researchers, but within the form and structure of the city are the private accumulations, the organic sub-soil of literate culture. These are the libraries of love and passion, brimful of manuscripts, pamphlets, old editions, and books marked and worn by life rather than by time alone.

A familiar sight in Edinburgh for many years was the tall gangling figure of Hamish Henderson, wandering between University and Sandy Bell's Bar, with the eponymous and beloved dog Sandy wandering in sympathy. Equally Hamish might cut out of the classical elegance of George Square to head for home across the Meadows, leafy or exposed according to the season. Regardless of temperature, however, this noted folklorist and cultural activist sported a capacious crinkly cardigan, largely unbuttoned.

Those inclined to smile on another Edinburgh eccentric knew nothing of Hamish Henderson's life experience or the library of passionate engagement which was breeding back in his top-floor Southside flat. That personal accumulation is now sadly dispersed yet faithfully catalogued by Carmen and Gordon Wright; its poetry and passions live on.

A play written by Henderson for the Cambridge Mummers in 1939 reminds us that this Perthshire Scot grew up in a decade of political conflict and disaster. *The Humpy Cromm* is set at Speakers Corner, allowing the working-class voices of Communists, Irish Nationalists, Spanish Republicans and British Fascists to be heard in discordant chorus. The struggle against Fascism was to swallow the best years of his youth, but not without protest.

In the library the Spanish poet Lorca was a significant presence:

because we want our daily bread
alder flower and perennial threshed tenderness,
because we want the will of the Earth to be fulfilled
that yields up its fruits for all of us

Translated from Lorca's 'El poeta in Nueva York' by Paul Pinding

Thirty and forty years later Henderson was still celebrating Lorca and explicitly connecting him to Scotland. The *duende* or indefinable artistic power which Lorca perceived in Andalucían *cante jondo* became equivalent to the conyach acknowledged by the Scottish Travellers as the ground of their ballad-singing art, without which even a superb voice was hollow. It was not the text, the music, the performer or the audience that counted but what happened between them. Like Lorca, Henderson was never content with the mere publication of poetry.

I heard those lectures and I have the articles on my sprawling shelves. I have also memorably heard Sheila Stewart, the Scottish Traveller, sing in the conviction of conyach. Yet perhaps Henderson's commentary would have lacked its carrying power had he not found his own poetic voice. The young Henderson, now a Cambridge graduate in modern languages, went to wartime service with the 51st Highland Division first in the North African desert and then in Italy. His *Elegies for the Dead in Cyrenaica* are among the great poems of the Second World War – Scottish, European, and universal:

> *There were our own, there were the others.*
> *Therefore, minding the great word of Glencoe's*
> *son, that we should not disfigure ourselves*
> *with villainy of hatred; and seeing that all*
> *have gone down like curs to anonymous silence,*
> *I will bear witness for I knew the others.*
> *Seeing that littoral and interior are alike indifferent*
> *and the birds are drawn again to our welcoming north*
> *why should I not sing **them**, the dead, the innocent?*

Hamish Henderson, *Elegies for the Dead in Cyrenaica*

It is easy to forget the post-war impact of those poems because other aspects of Henderson's muse were to sound out so vibrantly. My slim copy of *Elegies* sits alongside the expansive *Collected Poems and Songs* produced by Raymond Ross and published in Edinburgh in 2000. There was an 80th birthday ceilidh in the Old Town and, if truth be told, the elderly poet remained impassive to the voicing of elegies, but came to life at the sound of lyrics which he had brilliantly conceived for the popular sung tradition:

Then fare weel ye banks o Sicily,
Fare ye weel ye valley and shaw.
There's nae Jock will mourn the kyles o ye
Puir bliddy sqaddies are wearie.

Hamish Henderson, *Collected Poems and Songs*

Or one that gained the supreme accolade of 'Anonymous'
penned by Henderson to 'Lili Marlene':

We are the D-Day Dodgers, out in Italy –
Always on the vino, always on the spree.
8th Army scroungers and their tanks
We live in Rome – among the yanks.
We are the D-Day Dodgers, way out in Italy.

Hamish Henderson, *Collected Poems and Songs*

These songs still echo in Edinburgh, in Scotland and elsewhere,
but the library reveals a complex underweave of reflection and
purpose. Henderson witnessed at first hand the resistance
movement in Italy and the struggle to renew the left in post-
war conditions. When the prison letters of Antonio Gramsci,
the Communist leader who suffered ten years of incarceration
under Mussolini's tyranny, were published in 1947, Hamish
Henderson was the first to translate them into English. Here
was a radical political vision that recognised the importance of
popular culture and the national dimension.

That was Europe, but was Scotland part of the European
dynamic? The library demonstrates Henderson's closeness
to the Scottish Renaissance movement. Beside Gramsci was
the libretto of Erik Chisholm's Celtic Opera *Isles of Youth.*

Chisholm championed modern music in Glasgow at a time when J.D. Fergusson, dance artist Margaret Morris, publisher William MacLellan, poet Hugh MacDiarmid, and many others were creating a genuinely international movement in Scottish culture. Hamish Henderson became part of this movement but he brought his own distinctive contribution – art that was international, unrecognised and owned by the marginalised and oppressed.

The clues for Henderson were the songs of the 8th Army and the Italian partisans, Gramsci's Sardinian roots, and the work of the Irish Folklore Commission which had employed Calum MacLean to record Scottish Gaelic oral tradition. He took the road, beginning in his native Perthshire, to discover the extent of surviving folksong in Scotland. The result was, in his own image, like holding a tin pail under a waterfall.

Travelling people, crofters, agricultural labourers, former soldiers, and shepherds opened hearts and minds to Henderson and MacLean revealing an unsuspected treasury of artistic wealth and performative power. But Hamish's further political inspiration was to bring this scattered work of cultural survival home to Scotland's capital city, both in the founding of the School of Scottish Studies at Edinburgh University and in the Peoples Ceilidhs of 1951 and 1952. In this grand riposte to the Edinburgh International Festival trade unionists, the despised 'tinkers', and Gaelic tradition-bearers united to give public voice to what had previously been heard only within their own communities.

Edinburgh was not accustomed to such outbursts of radical passion and took notice. The city inclined solidly to order and, in the axiom of Odysseus Elytis approvingly quoted by Henderson, 'whenever you hear about order start smelling human flesh.' The oppressive contrasts of the capital city – the gibbet and the reveller – were now harnessed to the engine of protest, upearthing burghal dead weight with folksong spiced by Hamish's personal poetics:

> *Reekie, tell me my true love's name.*
> *Edinburgh Castle, toun and tour*
> *The Gowans gay and the gilliefloor.*
> *Lovers daffin aneath the slae*
> *Floret silva undique*
> *The bonniest pair ye iver seen*
> *Fuckin aneath the flooerin' gean.*
> *Bairnies wankin abuin the clay*
> *Floret silva undique.*

Hamish Henderson, *Collected Poems and Songs*

In 1952 the Peoples Festival Committee was banned by the Edinburgh Labour Party. But by now Henderson was unstoppable.

A folk revival had begun but it was much more than an enthusiasm for folksong, and the nature of the more is revealed in Hamish Henderson's library. Firstly there was the international scholarship positioning the past and present study of Scottish traditions in the contexts of European and American Romanticism, African independence movements, and worldwide literature. Hamish's one-volume ready reference edition of Francis James Child's *English and Scottish Popular Ballads* has now migrated from his shelves to mine. It is a well-thumbed, hard-worked book which Henderson radically reinterpreted through his knowledge of living folksong. Child's international classic has never been read in the same way since Henderson.

Secondly, or equally, there are the links to contemporary politics in Scotland and beyond. The folksong revival spun into CND, the anti-Polaris campaign, industrial protests and attacks on absentee landlords. Amongst the volumes of Henderson's passions and protests is the 1951 printed version of Ewan McColl's *Uranium 235* dedicated to Joan Littlewood and introduced by MacDiarmid. This 'documentary play' was performed to huge audiences in Scotland and England, reinvigorating theatre as a political art, and paving the way for 7:84. Just as Gramsci's thinking opened up a possibility for Dario Fo in Italy, so the thinking behind the folk revival was to invade theatre in the 1970s to dramatic effect in John McGrath's *The Cheviot, the Stag and the Black, Black Oil.*

The stream of activism was then flowing freely from Henderson's library to mine, uniting culture and politics. There is an Edinburgh Festival Broadsheet of 1973 in which the founding father is focused on forward momentum: 'The revival will sink or swim by its capability to throw up new and constantly fresh thinkers and writers.' Then in 1979 came the re-established Edinburgh Folk Festival, the same year as the failed Devolution Referendum. It snowed across the city that Easter, but the passion came through. A major conference, themed 'The People's Past', explored the relationship between folk traditions and Scotland's disputed histories. The political ground was shifting in Scotland, but Hamish Henderson was not seeking a new consensual centre:

Folk, the Folk that matters, has always in fact something of the rebel underground about it; whether it be the love-songs which reject the values and prejudices of a money-minded bourgeois society, or a hypocritical puritan religious set-up; the bawdy songs which frankly rejoice in the fun and comedy of sex; the 'Ding Dong Dollar' CND songs which pillory the antics of military bigwigs and the bonzes of imperialist power politics; the 'Sangs of the Stane' which send up the pretensions and absurdities of a stuffy royalist Establishment; the bothy songs which put on record the cheese-paring niggardliness of skinflint farmers – all share to a greater or lesser extent this rebel élan.

Hamish Henderson, 'It was in You That it A' Began'

Later that same year Odysseus Elytis won the Nobel Prize for Literature, and the Greek students in Edinburgh threw a party. At the centre of the action they put Hamish Henderson as both ceilidh master and a superb reader of Elytis translations. I still have the hand-stitched booklet produced for the occasion, as did Henderson, but more important is the experience of Edinburgh transformed for one night into a true Athens of the north by this mantic declamation:

> *Here then am I,*
> *created for the young Korai and the Aegean islands,*
> *lover of the deer's leaping,*
> *initiate in the Mystery of olive leaves,*
> *sun-drinker and locust-killer.*
> *Here am I, face to face*
> *with the black shirts of the ruthless*
> *and of the years' empty belly that aborted*
> *its own children, in heat!*

Odysseus Elytis, *The Axiom Esti*

To the Italian patriot then must be added the Hellenist, but still above all the apostle of Eros, 'I'll unleash the old kisses canonized by my longing!'

The Henderson library reaffirms that with its attachment to the Alexandrian poet C.P. Cavafy, who brings us geographically full circle to the North African elegies. Disappointment is a word not easily associated with Hamish Henderson, yet the ageing radical had to thole 17 further years of political stagnation in Scotland and the inevitable institutionalisation of his brainchild, the School of Scottish Studies. The path to Sandy Bell's and the company of a new generation of enthusiasts brought congenial compensations, but it was Cavafy who offered consolation:

As you go on the journey to Ithaca,
Pray that your way may be a long one,
Full of adventures, full of knowledge,
Do not be afraid of Poseidon's anger,
The Cyclops or the Laestrygonians,
You will never find such things upon your journey
If your thoughts remain lofty, and if a fine
Feeling has touched your body and your soul …

Always have Ithaca at the back of your mind.
The arrival there is your objective.
But do not be in any hurry on your journey.
Better to let it last for years.
In old age you will anchor at the island,
Rich with all you have gained upon the way,
Not expecting Ithaca to give you riches.

Translated from Cavafy's 'Ithaca' by Robert Liddell

Hamish Henderson's library has been scattered now, but his voices live on in the city of loves and passions. We store them on new shelves and in new minds and voices. One of the poet's songs is the unofficial anthem of a new devolved Scotland, 'The Freedom Come-All-Ye', though for Henderson the Scottish Parliament is a milestone but not the final destination of an independent socialist country.

So come all ye at hame wi Freedom,
Never heed whit the hoodies croak for doom.
In your hoose a' the bairns o Adam
Can find breid, barley-bree and painted room.
When MacLean meets wi's freens in Springburn
A' the roses and geans will turn tae bloom,
And a black boy frae yont Nyanga
Dings the fell gallows o the burghers doon.

Hamish Henderson, *Collected Poems and Songs*

Aspiration and protest join to affirm not what is but what should and could be. But the tone is ringing not shrill or hectoring. That is because the library has a ground note beneath its many variations. You catch it I think in an early Henderson poem, based on Holderlin:

He who has thought the most loves the fullest of life;
Highest virtue is prized by him who has looked on the world;
And often the wisest turn
To beauty in the end of all.

Hamish Henderson, *Collected Poems and Songs*

That is an apt epitaph for Henderson, fit to be inscribed on the stones of Edinburgh UNESCO City of Literature, but it is also a declaration of love. *The Collected Poems and Songs* has pride of place on my bookshelves, because it speaks to heart and mind. 'And often the wisest turn to beauty in the end of all.'

The Halcyon Days of Singers

Andrew R.C. Hamilton

The Singer Sewing Machine Company built a factory in Scotland in the 19th century, in Bridgeton, Glasgow; then, in 1882, it moved to Clydebank in Dunbartonshire where a mammoth factory was built. The area is now the Clydebank Business Park housing a variety of small businesses which contrast dramatically with the enormity of the Singer factory complex.

At its peacetime peak some 16,000 men and women worked there. The only feature which survives is Singer Railway Station, but many memories remain with the Clydebank people, especially Singers workers, no matter where they now live. Both domestic and industrial sewing machines were manufactured and when I write 'manufactured' I mean exactly that, for virtually every part of the machine and its wooden cabinet housing was made in the Clydebank plant. The factory was the basic source of income for many families. The population of Clydebank at its peak was around 50,000 and, in most families, someone worked in the factory. There seemed to be more women than men but that could have been an illusion. All the women were single or widowed. When a girl married she had to give up her job. If a woman was widowed, she could be considered for re-employment. Divorcees, if any could be found, need not have applied.

Into the factory, trains came rolling with workers from all airts and pairts of Glasgow and its surrounds. There were seven lines leading into the marshalling yard which was called Singers Lie and now houses Clydebank Shopping Centre. Work started each weekday, including Saturday, at 8.00 am with a horn blowing firstly at five minutes to eight to remind stragglers to hurry, then on the hour to say 'Now lads, and lasses, let's go, another day, another opportunity to make good money.' No one in Clydebank had any difficulty in knowing the time of day for the horns blew and the four faces of the giant clock were visible from every part of the town. Inside the grounds of the factory there were two puffer trains, owned by Singers, which plied within the factory grounds on 25 miles of track. These trains were used to move the raw pig iron from the Lie to the foundry, to move all sorts of material, and parts during manufacture, and to take, eventually, the finished machines from the factory into the Lie for delivery worldwide.

Many of the girls who went into the factory, straight from school, took one look at the place and wondered if they could settle. They may well have thought this doubtful. Apprehension would increase when they were given the usual one week to learn how to operate their allotted machine in, say, the veneering section of the cabinet shop. In the tradition of the place, the girl currently working the machine would be the one to give instruction. If a girl overcame that feeling of strangeness and imprisonment, or at least of being shut up for the day, she would be absorbed into the fraternity of her department and, more than likely, she would stay there until she married.

It was possible to identify many Singer workers from their body odour. They smelt of oil from the lubricant used to ensure that the materials being machined could be more easily worked. This was true but not applicable to workers in departments in which wood or cast iron was being machined. The wood department (the cabinet shop) was relatively clean, but it could be difficult to see clearly in the areas where the cast iron parts of the sewing machines were being shaped because cast iron is machined dry. There was a haze of fine, cast iron particles floating in the atmosphere, being deposited on the skins and probably in the lungs of the workers. At the end of a shift they looked like coal miners.

A distinctive culture was built up over the years, a feeling by employees of belonging to an institution, particularly if they had been there most of their working lives. This was assisted by Singers being as near to a self-contained industrial entity as one could imagine. It was geared to making everything associated with the product. To do so there were three major factories within the factory. These were the foundry, the cabinet shop and the parts manufacturing area. The largest section was given over to parts manufacture by machining, most of which was done on automatic machines. These were machines which, once set, went through the same cycle, time after time, producing the same parts to within the same limits of accuracy. And these machines were designed and built within the factory.

The feeling of identity within the company was aided by the many leisure activities catered for. There was a pipe band which competed at the highest level, striving to become world champions at the Dunoon Highland Games every year. There was a brass band, hockey pitches, bowling greens, tennis courts, and an athletic sports and football ground. And there was Singers Hall, a beautiful spacious building. Every Friday evening in winter, public dancing to a four or five-piece band was held in the main hall, a mecca for young lads to meet young girls in near-perfect conditions. Seeds were sown and many a romance blossomed at these dances. The hall was not noted for hooliganism but for the decorum shown. It was the traditional way by which the young of both sexes met in a wholesome environment.

June was the month for the annual gala and sports meeting for which a queen was selected and crowned. Aspiring and proven athletes competed in the track events. It was an event to which everyone in Clydebank looked forward, whether or not they worked in Singers. Those who enjoyed success in the competitions proudly displayed their winnings to their workmates on the following Monday morning, and held on to their medals for a lifetime. The girls loved the gala days, the beautiful frocks worn by the queen and her 20 to 30 attendants. In keeping with the factory philosophy of self-reliance, these frocks were made on the premises on Singer sewing machines.

In the 1930s, Singers had factories in France, Italy and Germany. Each of these were in direct competition with the Clydebank plant but not seen in these terms by the Clydebank workers. Consequently, they were happy to pick a football team to play against these foreign plants. International football was, therefore, another Singer recreational activity. More often than not, Clydebank were victorious.

One of the departments employing mainly women was the needle, or No.19, department. The term 'department' is used for clarity, but it was actually known as 'the needle flat' – almost a factory within itself. To produce a needle from a coil of wire required 16 operations including pointing, eye polishing, and straightening. To straighten each needle a little machine hammer came down on the surface at exactly the correct weight and pressure. It was not uncommon for a girl to work up to seven machines simultaneously. Perhaps it would be more correct to say that she supervised seven machines. Usually, a tradesman would set these machines and the girl operator would then be responsible for feeding in the part-finished needles and for seeing that there was no hitch in the processing of each needle.

Production workers were paid so much per hundred, known as piece work. No production, no wages. If a girl had a good week, she could come home with around £2 in wages. Girls were always paid less than men.

In one department small electric motors were manufactured. Officially, this was No. 47 department but throughout the factory it was known as 'the beauty parlour'. It was eminently suitable for girls, being clean and requiring manual dexterity rather than strength. Years earlier, the manager had established the practice of engaging only lovely-looking lassies. In spite of that handicap, the girls were good at their work.

The factory was closed in 1979. The loss of the factory was a body blow to many families in Clydebank, in surrounding towns and in Glasgow.

Why did Singers close this factory?

Some folk consider it was lack of profitability. A drop of some 10 per cent to 20 per cent in sales was too much for the factory to cope with. The sewing machine was no longer part of the furniture in most households It had gone the same way as the family piano, overtaken by the tide of events, the changes in demand and fashion. Others realised that the old production machinery still in use would have to be replaced at high capital cost. And the buildings which had stood for nearly 100 years required renovation. The company tried making irons and various cleaners but none was a suitable and viable replacement for the sewing machine.

To be philosophical one might say that everything has a life span: things are born, live and die. Factories follow that pattern and Singers was no exception. Well, we might be right. On the other hand, the explanation could be that I had left the factory some years before it closed. They must have missed me badly!

The Bank, the Well and the Cross

Rene Anderson

Ruthwell is a gey dreich place in winter. As soon as the young folk have gone off to work in nearby towns and the old folk have retreated behind their net curtains to sit at the fireside, the village is deserted. The odd tractor plies up and down the main street with food for the beasts, which are kept indoors during the long winter months. Even the sheep huddle behind the hedges when they are not munching the frozen neeps that sustain them through this time of year. The proximity to the Solway Firth should suggest a mild climate but by the time the wind and driving rain sweep across the flat land the trees are bent double.

The village itself has little to commend it. Any aim of planners to preserve some of its early character failed spectacularly once the idea of designating Ruthwell a conservation area was abandoned in the 1980s. Two hundred years ago the Earl of Mansfield had the higgledy-piggledy cottages laid out in a straight line. Today there are still no pavements. There are street lights, although one only has to walk a few yards to escape their pollution and to see the spectacular night skies. On the face of it, Ruthwell seems an unlikely setting for three of the most important historic sites in the country. Perhaps its main charm is that there is no soulless chain hotel, restaurant or even an information centre. The visitor can search for the jewels, unimpeded by neon signs or advertisements. The ubiquitous boring brown signs give no hint of the treasures to be unearthed.

At the bottom of the village a neat, whitewashed cottage houses the Savings Banks Museum, the very building where in 1810 the Rev. Henry Duncan DD opened the world's first savings bank based on business principles. In a community of starving parishioners, he underwrote a cargo of corn to feed the people and then taught them how to save for their future. The modest funds – £151 for the first year – were placed with the Linen Bank in Dumfries and made five per cent interest. Members received four per cent interest – on whole pounds. The surplus paid for administration and for a charity fund. It also provided tiered interest for long-term savers. The savings bank movement spread throughout the country and beyond. Although savings banks now employ millions of people all over the world, Airdrie remains the sole survivor of the movement in Scotland.

Records show that in this wee cottage, male members of the Friendly Society met, occasionally drank ale and ate cheese, listened to music and read the local newspaper, of which Henry Duncan was editor and owner. Duncan even imported news from London about the Napoleonic Wars for his *Dumfries & Galloway Courier*. As supervisor of the parish school, he made sure that all pupils could read, even though most of their parents probably could not. Once a year, female members were allowed to take tea in the Society room, a tiny but significant advance for women, which spread throughout the land as 'kirk soirées'.

Although recent updating of the museum may have detracted somewhat from the atmosphere, there is still much to recommend it. It is easy to imagine the parishioners trudging wearily down the street from the fields on a Saturday evening to entrust to their minister the few pennies they could spare from their meagre earnings. Even during harvesting they would finish work early on Saturday evening, in order to prepare for the Sabbath when no work would be done.

In the entrance to the Society room there is an exhibition of savings boxes from all over the country. Other bank memorabilia, including an international collection of coins, notes and passbooks, are laid out attractively in glass cases, while panels round the wall tell the history of the savings bank movement and the life of the remarkable Henry Duncan. The prize exhibit is the wee green tin box in which the first modest savings were collected. Duncan's beeswax model of the Ruthwell Cross is particularly noteworthy. Also on display is a sample of the first fossil footprints in Britain, identified by Duncan. A look beyond the exhibition provides an insight into the entire social history of the parish. The massive old bank ledgers show that many families with the same name still reside in the parish. The bank records, as well as books, photographs, estate papers and a modest but important collection of manuscripts, are a rich resource for genealogy enthusiasts and historians alike.

On the outskirts of Ruthwell village is the Brow Well, a chalybeate spring whose restorative waters attracted many visitors over the centuries. Although for the past few decades the water has been classed as undrinkable, visitors still seek out this unremarkable place, for it was here that our national bard, Robert Burns, spent the last few weeks of his short life, in a vain attempt to cure himself of the illness which was to prove fatal. The Saltire flies over the spot and a bench has been placed for visitors to rest while contemplating the demise of such genius. Each July, on the anniversary of his death, several hundred people gather round for a service led by the local minister. Passages from the Bible in Scots are read, hymns sung and a lone piper plays a lament. Sometimes the sun beats down on the gathering; at other times the chill wind and driving rain are sad reminders of what this sick man might have suffered, bathing up to his neck in the chilly waters of the Solway Firth. It's a sad, poignant place, at times completely submerged, when high tides and poor weather coincide.

Whilst Burns was at the Brow Well, he was invited to Ruthwell Manse by the Rev. John Craig, whose daughter Agnes was later to marry Henry Duncan. It was to Agnes, who closed the curtains to block out the sun, that Burns supposedly uttered the words 'Let it shine. It hasnae lang to shine on me.' He died a few days after returning to Dumfries. Duncan never forgot the occasion when he met both Burns and the poet, Thomas Blacklock, at the manse at Lochrutton.

On his way to Ruthwell Manse, Burns might well have wandered through the kirkyard and noticed fragments of a moss-covered carved stone lying outside the kirk, a victim of the zealots of the Reformation, who had regarded it as an idolatrous monument and ordered it to be struck down. The poet would not have known that he was looking at the longest surviving Anglo-Saxon poem, carved on what was to become the most-discussed medieval object in western Europe – the 8th-century Ruthwell Cross.

Over a period of years, Henry Duncan gathered together the pieces of stone and erected the cross in the manse garden, where it was to remain till late in the century, when the Rev. James M'Farlan built an apse in the church and supervised the mammoth task of moving the stone inside and lowering it into the sunken area prepared for it. There it stands today, the warm sandstone changing colour as the light shines through the stained glass and down from the roof windows.

The four sides of the cross depict images and text from the Vulgate Bible, as well as the words of the poem, 'The Dream of the Rood'. Where this 18-foot preaching cross came from and how it ended up in Ruthwell are questions which have puzzled experts from all over the world. Theologians come to interpret the religious message, antiquarians come to assess its place in history, Freemasons puzzle over the symbols and geologists attempt to identify the source of the sandstone. Others come just to see a magnificent monument in a tiny church and to wonder at the skill and faith of the men who worked on it. Scholarly works and theories abound on this ancient cross. It remains one of the great mysteries of the world.

In Ruthwell village, when the fierce winds die down and spring gradually turns to summer, the lush green pastures become the playing fields of the lambs and the air is filled with their bleating. Tiny calves wobble alongside their mothers and sometimes take a few daring steps away from them. Cattle which have been cooped up all winter are sometimes seen stampeding down the village, kicking their heels in their search for the first fresh grass. Romany horses, with their big feet and piebald coats, stand protectively in the fields beside their foals. Soon the keen gardeners are out in the village, planting, mowing and cutting hedges. The dejected air has disappeared, out come the hanging baskets and tubs and the village gradually becomes a riot of colour. Neighbours who have not seen each other all winter are out in the street chatting and discussing their entry for the village-in-bloom contest. Ruthwell won again this year.

Croy Parish Church

Rev. Jan Mathieson, Croy Parish Church, Mrs McArthur,
Andrew Macdonald, Mrs Christine McLean and
Primary 6/7 Croy Primary School

The building of Croy Parish Church began in 1764 and was completed in 1767. High up in one of the gables is a stone inscription that reads '17 TM 67'. Before the church was built, people probably came to the same place to worship, maybe in a round chapel.

Important monied families in the area had a responsibility to help build the church. Plaques in honour of members of these families hang on the church walls. There are three sections upstairs, in what is called the 'loft', set aside for members of these families to sit on plush seats during the service. The wealthy folk did not need to come in the church door, they entered via the loft door. The lower level of the church was occupied by the other folk of the parish who sat on hard seats.

The minister had the glebe, which was land around the church, to keep sheep to make a livelihood. The Church Hall was originally the steading where the minister kept his livestock – cattle and ponies (for transport). It was converted during 1970–1980 into a Church Hall. The minister was given a house (manse) around 1851. The men building the manse, whilst on the roof, saw the first steam train pass by from Inverness to Nairn.

In Scotland, members of the congregation formed a committee to choose a new minister. In 1820, the Rev. Alexander Campbell was chosen as the new minister of Croy Church by the wealthy families of Cawdor. This caused a riot. Some 1,500 people gathered at the churchyard and threw mud and stones at the minister before chasing him as far as Tornagrain. A solicitor, along with the Captain of the Guard, was brought to deal with this riot. They read the Riot Act which at that time was a real piece of paper saying 'Go home or be arrested.' Later, people changed their minds about the minister and he went on to preach in the church for 29 years. In 1833, however, two men broke into the minister's garden, stealing a beehive. They were later charged.

In the beginning, the pulpit was probably in the centre of the church. The font, dating back to 1873, was gifted by a teacher called James Falconer, who had worked at Croy School for 50 years. The bookstand was given in memory of Charles Fraser, a past minister of the church. The offering used to be collected in a 'ladle' and care had to be taken in passing it around in case the money fell out!

Many of the graves in the churchyard are from the 18th century. However, the oldest grave found was dated 1661 and the oldest upright grave dates back to 1732. The new graves are separated from the old graves, with the graves of ministers being close to the church. In Victorian times, grave robbers were common. To stop grave robbers from digging up newly made graves, watchers would have to keep watch whenever a new grave was made.

St Kilda: Returning Home to the Edge of the World

John Morrison

As the pilot presses a button which brings the helicopter engines to life with a roar, Norman John Gillies positions a set of headphones carefully over his ears and adjusts the microphone in front of his mouth. He turns to three middle-aged passengers in the seat behind him, smiles broadly, gives a thumbs up and shouts, 'St Kilda here we come.'

Bridget, Shirley and John can all hear him through their own headsets. They are sharing a unique experience. It is the eve of the 75th anniversary of the evacuation of St Kilda and for the first time the Gillies family are going back to their father's birthplace.

The 41-mile journey from Benbecula to St Kilda is a short hop by helicopter and within minutes of departure the pilot points out some rocks, jutting directly skywards, on the horizon. Norman John and his wife Ivy see them immediately. He knows exactly where to look in the vast ocean opening out below and he guides her eyes with an outstretched hand. Their son and daughters lean towards a side window, craning their necks. They cannot see anything at first, but seconds later their excited shouts come through the interconnected headphones.

This is their first sighting of a place they have wanted to visit since they heard of St Kilda on their father's knee.

Overhead, the sky is blue but further out the islands' high cliffs act like a magnet for the clouds that have raced, unimpeded, for thousands of miles across the north Atlantic. As the helicopter approaches, St Kilda looms larger, the land dark against the blue sea, the hilltops enveloped in a white cumulus cloud which gives the impression that you are approaching another world.

The pilot's calm voice comes through the headphones. John MacKenzie is a veteran of the skies around the Hebrides, regularly conveying men and supplies to the radar station on this, the furthest outpost of the British Isles. He explains the landing routine and apologises in advance for any bumps on the approach but the passengers are too excited to worry. They can see Hirta, Soay, Boreray, Stac an Armin, names which have become so familiar through the stories told and retold by their father.

Minutes later the helicopter touches down safely. The engines are switched off, the rotor blades begin to slow down and finally stop. Norman John is the first to emerge, walking gingerly across the rocky ground, shoes in hand. He was unable to put them on in Benbecula after struggling into an awkward sea survival suit with such tightly fitting rubber attachments around the neck and wrist that they threaten to cut off the blood supply to his head and hands. In his earlier life, Norman John would not have worn shoes. The leathery skin on his young feet was so tough that no rock made him wince.

The rest of the family quickly join him, all looking equally uncomfortable in their survival suits. Looking up towards the deserted village, Norman John shouts into the wind, 'We are here. I bet you didn't think you'd see the day. I'm so happy to be back in my small island home.'

The questions come so quickly he is unable to answer them: 'Which house was yours?' 'Can we really go inside it?' 'Where did you play?' 'Where is the school?' 'Where is the church?'

A small group of workers have made their way around the bay from the radar station to watch the arrival. They are mostly laid-back Gaelic speakers from the neighbouring Western Isles. Over the years they have watched, with wry amusement, many excited visitors overcome by the aura, mystery and the almost physical impact of stepping onto St Kilda. But they know this group is different. Norman John is a St Kildan. He is the last remaining son of the island, a living link with a civilisation which stretched back to the Bronze Age. He has come home.

The Gillieses are shepherded into a small grey Portakabin with two benches and about 20 hooks for hanging survival suits. There is a notice on the door – International Air and Sea Terminal. Clearly, you need a good sense of humour to survive the winter here.

It takes a lot less time to get out of a survival suit than into it and the family are soon walking up the grassy slope towards the houses. Every step evokes a memory for Norman John. Turning round to face the sea, he points to the black, jagged cliffs that protrude from the waves like giant's teeth guarding Village Bay and tells of two uncles who were drowned in 1909 when their boat was ambushed by a squally sea on the way back from a fishing trip. Norman John's grandfather survived by clinging to the rocks. His desperate cries were heard above the storm in the village and another boat was dispatched to bring him back to safety.

Genealogy is important in places like this and the next baby boy born into the family has carried the names of the two men, Norman and John, into another century. That boy, now 80 years old, explains why he was never called Norman. Or John. He was always Norman John, or Tormod Iain, in the native Gaelic language of the islanders. Both names given equal status. Both lives equally remembered.

The houses of the last inhabitants still stand, huddled in a crescent shape along what the islanders called 'The Street'. Behind them the highest hill, Conachair, rises sharply for 1,400 feet like a protective sentry before plunging dramatically back down to the sea. This is the highest sea cliff in Britain and it gave some shelter from the worst ravages of the Atlantic storms.

The slope down towards Village Bay is gentler. The rocks that divided each family plot, which ran from the house to the sea, are still visible. This is where the crops that helped sustain the islanders and their animals through the long winter were cultivated. The brown Soay sheep, survivors from the Bronze Age and unique to St Kilda, are still grazing here, undisturbed. One of the most primitive breeds in the world. they are smaller than most other sheep but much hardier. They have to be.

Norman John leads his family through the village. Although 75 years have passed since he was evacuated along with 35 other inhabitants his memory is still sharp. He can recall the family names from each house, the number of children they had, and which part of the world they were scattered to. Norman MacKinnon, his wife and eight children lived at No. 1. Finlay MacQueen lived alone at No. 2. No one had lived in No. 3 since 1924 when William MacDonald, his wife and eight children had moved to Leverburgh in Harris before settling in Stornoway.

Pointing to an empty space between two houses he tells them, 'This is the Post Office.' He uses the present tense although the outline of where the corrugated-iron shack once stood is all that remains. At the next house he stops again, 'I used to come down here to play.'

As Bridget, Shirley and John look around them in awe and amazement everything they see begs a question. 'What are the dome-shaped stone buildings that are dotted around the island? There must be hundreds of them.' Their father explains that this was the St Kildan fridge. The 'cleits' vary in size but most are about 10 feet in diameter and about 5 feet in height. They were ingeniously constructed with each stone selected according to its shape and size. The building tapers inwards to form the roof which is closed with bigger, heavier stones and was once protected from the rain by a covering of turf which has long gone. Gaps left in the walls allowed the ever-present wind to blow through freely to preserve all their produce – sea birds, eggs, hay, corn and turf for the fires. Most of the cleits are close to the houses but they can also be found on the neighbouring islands where they would be have been used by hunting parties culling sea birds.

Eventually, Norman John reaches house No. 10. He places his right hand against the gable end which no longer supports a roof, bows his head slightly and then, slowly, turns to face the rest of the family, 'This is my home. This is where I was born.'

It is an emotional moment for all of them. His three children, who were brought up in Ipswich close to Chatham Barracks where Norman John was stationed in 1945 and where he met his wife Ivy, have all seen photographs of St Kilda and heard the stories. In an instant, their father's early years are not being gleaned from sepia prints or developed by their own imagination after hearing his stories. They are seeing and touching for themselves.

Norman John takes a few steps forward and turns into the doorway of his first home. Walking inside, he points to the end wall on his right, 'The two bedrooms were here.' Bridget is shocked, 'What? No privacy, Dad?' Dad smiles. His children are seeing where his life began but he will never expect them to fully grasp what and where he came from.

Turning to his left, Norman John walks towards the other gable end, leans down and looks up through the hole where the hearth used to be. 'This,' he tells them, 'is where my mother did the baking and cooking. Scones, oatcakes, puffins.'

This was the staple diet of the islanders. It's reckoned every person on the island ate at least 100 fulmars every year along with a large number of gannets and puffins. The family have heard many, many times about the huge St Kildan appetite for sea birds but it still makes them laugh out loud.

The mood changes when Norman John stands at the stone-framed window which looks down to the sea. He pokes his hand through the gap where the glass used to be and speaks in a voice choking with a raw, rasping emotion that has not been diluted by the decades, 'These are very precious memories to me. I can still see her standing there on the wall calling me in Gaelic, "Tormod Iain thig dhachaigh gu do bhiadh." Norman John come home to your tea.' As the tears well up in his eyes, the old man is left alone for a few moments with his memories.

Norman John lost his mother before he reached school age. In January 1930 Mary Gillies, who was pregnant, became seriously ill. A passing fishing boat carried a message to the mainland requesting medical aid but a boat did not leave from Tarbert in Harris until 15 February. Norman John can still recall how his mother stood on deck, wrapped in her white shawl, waving goodbye as this boat moved slowly out of the bay. He never saw her again. Help had come too late.

The death certificate tells us Mary Gillies died in Stobhill

Hospital in Glasgow on 26 May because of a blood clot and abscess on her lung. The baby she was carrying had been delivered by Caesarean section 13 days earlier. Little Annie passed away the same day as her mother. Norman John does not know to this day where his mother was buried. He did not find out that he had a little sister until 1991 when his own son John started researching the family history.

The death of a young woman and her baby had a devastating effect on the confidence of the remaining islanders. It reinforced their feeling of isolation and of increasing helplessness in emergencies. That spring no crops were planted on the island. Evacuation, which had been considered on several previous occasions, had become inevitable.

After walking through the village, the Gillies family are keen to explore the rest of the island. One of the workers at the radar station arrives with a Land Rover and offers to take them up the narrow, winding, military road which almost reaches the summit of Conachair. It is a terrifying helter-skelter ride for the unfamiliar. The nonchalance of the driver, who goes up and down several times a day, seems to add to the unease of the Gillies family. At the side of the road on the right, the hill plunges downwards for hundreds of feet towards the deserted village. There are no crash barriers. A vehicle going over the side would disintegrate long before it would stop rolling. But for thousands of years St Kildans had to walk up here to collect turf for the fire and sea birds for dinner.

At the summit, while the rest of the family come to terms with the wind which is considerably stronger than below, Norman John moves around as stealthily as one of the Soay sheep. The scenery is breathtaking. Landscape artists will tell you that it is difficult to recreate Scotland on canvas because the country seems to move at 3,000 mph. In St Kilda this can be multiplied by ten. The light changes every nanosecond. Showers appear from nowhere. Four miles away, Boreray is covered by a thick dark cloud which carries a heavy shower. Within seconds the downpour has moved on. Shafts of light appear through the cloud. The black cliffs are soon sparkling in the sunlight.

Norman John tells of feats of endurance which would embarrass the toughest soldiers in the SAS regiments. In the 1700s three men and eight boys went to Stac an Armin to collect gannets. While they were away, an outbreak of smallpox wiped out most of the population on the main island and no one was able to go to collect them. Somehow, they survived for nine months before being rescued. How often they must have looked across at Conachair and wondered what was happening down in the village on the other side. Conachair has stood above Village Bay since the volcanic eruptions which forced it up from the seabed many thousands of years ago. It bore witness to the arrival of the first Neolithic settlers. It saw times of plenty when the island supported a population of 200. And times of famine and disease when the islanders only survived because of outside help. In the early 20th century, it witnessed the slow death of St Kilda as the people gradually moved away to take advantage of better opportunities and an easier life on the mainland.

On a cold day in February 1930, Mary Gillies would have pressed against the rail of the ship until Conachair and the island where she had left her only child disappeared over the horizon. Its image must have been seared on her memory as she wept with the anguish of separation and the physical pain in her chest which would soon claim her life.

On a sunny day in August of the same year, when five-year-old Norman John and the other islanders were evacuated, they watched from the deck of the *Harebell* until the familiar outline of Conachair became faint and finally disappeared. Many of them wept. They knew they would not be back. The link between the people and the island was severed. An ancient civilisation had ceased to exist.

Seventy-five years later, on another fine day in August, Norman John Gillies, his wife, son and daughters stand on the brow of Conachair and pose for one final photograph for the album. It will take its place alongside the last photograph of Mary Gillies sitting outside No. 10. Norman John's children never met their grandmother, but her short life has shaped theirs. After smiling at the camera, the family move silently towards the Land Rover to go back down the hill where the helicopter is waiting for them.

Green Grow the Rashes, O

Hamish Gillies

'There must come a time,' said Dite, the farmer who is our neighbour, 'when we will give up borrowing money and work-ing hard to produce food that nobody wants.' Dite in these parts is the diminutive of David.

Farmers like most of us who work – with the possible excep-tion of lawyers – have always moaned about not being properly rewarded. My mother was a farmer's daughter and I had uncles in Angus and Ireland. I can remember those days when farmers had new Jaguars and more money than they knew what to do with.

At the beginning of the bad times, Dite had shrugged and said, 'If you're no canny, you don't survive, it's aye been like that. You pull the belt a notch tighter and don't buy anything … except of course the water of life.' Dite had al-ready diversified. He had chalets and Betty ran a small busi-ness in Denhead, our nearest village.

But when lambs were not worth a shotgun shell, he said, his windburnt face as grey as it could be, 'I'm thinking of applying for Income Support.' He is not old enough but in the weight of his words he could have been talking of the disgrace of needing the support of the Parish. He survived without Income Sup-port but keeping afloat is still a daily battle.

When I was young, my uncles seldom had to roll up their sleeves. Now Dite and his daughter Liz run four farms; farms that used to support four families and a dozen shepherds, cattlemen, tractormen, orramen and their families.

When I drive back to the glen from the city during hectic times – ploughing, lambing, calving, haying and the harvest – the hills are laced by the headlights of tractors.

Last summer, when we thought that we had become the rain capital of the universe, I was awakened early, just before four, by the absence of rain on the roof and the sound of Dite's tractor. 'I've made some hellish hay, but I've never made bad silage,' he later said to me. Nowadays, to make silage the hay is cut, rolled and sealed in airtight plastic. The rolls must be wrapped either within six hours, or two or three weeks, after cutting. If the main fermentation has begun before the rolls are wrapped, the rolls blow up and burst. Liz drove over from the other side of the glen and the pair cut till the evening. A contractor then wrapped the rolls of grass, the machine laying out the black plastic-covered rolls like eggs, or turds.

At three the following morning, I heard Dite and Liz stacking the rolls.

'If you leave them lying in the field,' Dite said, 'the beasts come along and think – Oh, what's this? I'll just hae a nibble – and of course they are no content with one roll but open them all up. The air gets in and it's ruined.'

It is easy for us city folk to believe that the countryside exists for our entertainment – a place to walk, hunt, fish, camp, or just to be soothed by its beauty. 'Do you see that over there, Peter?' Dite pointed at a field, about one third of an acre between neat dry-stone dykes. It was a maze of weeds and straggly young trees. 'Twenty years ago that was a market garden that supplied all the big houses and hotels in the glen. That's what the country will look like when we stop working.'

'Why do you keep going?'

He looked up at the hill dotted by his sheep and then down the glen. The river, full and glinty in the sun, turned and curved through the velvet green of the lower fields, between the new bright green of the silver birches and the dark olive green of the firs and pines. Dotted here and there were wee white houses and in the gardens flashes of the last of the daffodils and the first red rhododendrons. Less easily seen were the stone byres and steadings, farmhouses and the Admiral's big frowning house. The first oystercatchers trilled along the river; a couple of teuchats flapped their lazy dance in the cool spring air; high above a buzzard circled, screaming his cat-like cry; a couple of Dodd's new black lambs staggered beside their mother; a tractor roared as its wheels bit into the soft spring earth; and far away, a motorcycle changed gears at maximum revs.

The hillsides were brown with last year's bracken and heather, and patched with the brilliant mustard-yellow of the whins – such a beautiful colour, such jaggy points, such aggressive spread. The river turned and twisted and the sides of the glen grew steeper and steeper until it vanished into the Grampians still flecked with snow.

'Is it not bonny?' he said and smiled.

Christine

Jake Curley

Christine loved smoking; unfortunately it was not reciprocal.
I was informed she was only allowed two cigarettes per session. Sitting in her presence it soon became crystal clear why
this was so. Every five to ten minutes she would be coughing
her lungs up; a raking, rasping, reverberating cough, monumental and quite frightening really. However, like a fellow
addict, as soon as she had regained her composure she would
doe-eye my Benson and Hedges packet. And more often than
not I would relent and let her take a cigarette. The first session
with her went very well. She did a painting. She was great
really. There was no pissing about trying to draw everything
first. Colour was applied almost immediately. Even though we
used those crappy cakes of poster paint it was soon apparent
that she could use colour, really use it, get it working. It was
my second day working at the Project. Voluntary work one day
per week; on a Wednesday. The first week had gone well. I
wasn't sure what to expect. It was a mental health project. The
aim, and it had been achieved, was to create a safe working
environment, where clients could be creative. My job basically
was to help them with their art. The paintings and little sculp-
tures paraded around the place were testament to the fact that

this place worked. The effect on me was instant. As a way of settling in, I picked up some clay and started making a little igloo. And, well, for the first time since I had left art school a few years earlier, I was actually enjoying the experience. The main bonus about working here was the fact that although it was a small place, there were two places that you could smoke. One was downstairs in the basement. The sitting room was mainly used for meetings and art therapy sessions, one on one. The other place you could smoke was by the activities room window. So it was natural that I would gravitate to whoever was working at the activities room window. It was here that I met Christine.

She was an immensely powerful-looking woman dressed in men's clothes. She had the face of a female Russian hammer thrower who had caught her fanny hairs in a mangle at the very peak of premenstrual tension. Instantly making any man, whatever his opinion, concur with the slogan 'zero tolerance'. I had seen her many times before, correction, avoided her many times before. Living in the heart of the old town you could not help but notice her. Sometimes moving slowly, mostly sitting on benches or doorways. Her favourite spot was the steps at Jericho House. My boss introduced us. Christine put out a large reddish mitt, which I shook. Christine uttered the words 'Hiya darlin' in the sweetest little-girl voice I have ever heard. The voice of a child who had said something so cute, yet really deeply profound. A female version of Steinbeck's *Of Mice and Men*, Lon Channey in drag, beckoned me to take a pew. And, as my arse slipped onto the chair, I had seen the blueprint for her entire life. This big lumbering lump that was so fragile. Somebody who was so easy to use and abuse, something to be bullied. Those two words of greeting had shown me how appearances can be deceptive. Two childlike words over informative. Could there be malice lurking in that gingerbread core. I mean if a con man looks like a con man then he will be a very poor con man.

The scene was a farming landscape. Green rolling hills with a convoy of little white cottages travelling over them. When I asked where it was she informed me that it was Gorebridge. The place of her birth, where she grew up and where she yearned to be. The session was over, her painting pinned up for display. Soon she was reacquainted with her confiscated cigarettes and shuffling homewards to Jericho House.

During the debriefing session that followed, it was decided that we had both done rather well. I was told something of Christine's history. Chronic alcohol problems, incontinence which I had already deduced. Years and years of horrendous abuse. Three children taken from her in their infancy. That big flesh Henry Moore mother-figure never allowed to nurture. My mind switched off then. My own vivid fertile imagination seemed the easier softer route to be taken here. The bottom line is this – there was no hidden malice in this woman and I liked her. Liked her a lot if you want to know the truth.

Throughout the following Wednesday afternoon sessions we began working in clay. If her painting had impressed me, the way she worked with clay easily surpassed that, although it took some effort to get her started. When she got going she shifted. The initial reluctance to begin working was this – she also adored coffee. Coffee and cigarettes were a definite item. They rocked her world. Week by week she made either the face of a wee Highland man or a little cottage. The cottages always resembled Fred Flintstone dwellings with Tam O' Shanter roofs. The work was intricate, sort of Neolithic rococo style. I tried not to analyse it too much, but it slowly dawned on me that the way she worked clay was the way you worked pastry. These works transported me to her childhood, baking with the family in that Gorebridge farmhouse. The head of the household – that wee Highland man – cigarette in mouth walking through clouds of dusted flour, heading for the big kitchen table to await their culinary delights. And always in that wee man's head was the fact that as Christine grew, that big bad world drew nearer.

Sometimes when she worked she cried, and she cried gently for Gorebridge and her father. She was easy to placate, all you had to do was talk. She would say 'He doesn't want to know me' and I would try and explain that her father was very old and maybe was not up to seeing her at the moment. She accepted this the way she accepted everything that had befallen her. With her good and true heart, a dogged optimism shone through.

Another thing she could do well was lie. Some of the lies she told me were phenomenal. She would tell me she was going to get a new heart, a better one. The next week the doctors were going to cut her legs off. I knew by then that her doctors were only at the wind-up. I asked her how she was going to get about with no legs and she informed me she was going to get one of 'those scooterised wheelchair things'. When she traipsed in the next week you could see she was slightly miffed to be still on her pins. As the weeks turned to months, I learned more about her. She had christened me Joack by then; I still don't know if it was a pet name or an insightful comment. The Christmas party came and there she was in her element. She was cheating at 'Pass the Parcel' and doing really well at it. There was a glorious honesty about the way she held onto the object longer than anyone else. I was sitting there trying to hide the fact that I had won fuck all.

Then the day came when for no reason she burst out laughing. Mel Blanc, the voice of Bugs Bunny and many other cartoon characters, would have made millions more if he had perfected Christine's laugh. It was instantly infectious and extremely virulent. I immediately scanned the room. My thinking was this – it's a mental health project and there might be paranoid people, people thinking that she was laughing at them. I could not have been more wrong. The whole room was rocking. In fact staff were coming in from other rooms to join in the moment. They had heard it before and had probably been waiting for it to happen again the way you wait in the winter months for the day the sun tells you spring has sprung. Her laughter subsided amid heavy gasps of breath and little tiny sporadic laughs. Like a virtuoso's finishing flourish. That laugh remains inside me somewhere, something beautiful, something to be treasured.

Her incontinence was an ongoing problem and there were days when she had to be sent home early for a readjustment, so to speak. I had learned by then that her name for her private part was her 'thingy'. One day, and I'm sure she was suffering from a urine infection at the time, she stood up abruptly from the table and grabbed at herself in some pain. Her parting shot to me as she made her way to the bathroom was ' Ooh, ma thingy's stingy.' I tried hard to ignore her and even harder to keep a straight face.

It is by writing this piece that I have realised how the work she was doing influenced mine. All the time I had been there, I'd been making different types of clay dwellings. Then I decided to make a stone igloo. From this I moved onto ancient stone brochs made from pebbles I'd collected from the beach. Perfect scale replicas, I thought. People liked it and that led to me teaching a class in what was termed 'the Stone Project'. Despite sounding like a Charles Bronson movie, it went well. Trips to the beach were arranged for the collection of suitable stones. During some research, I guess looking for the big idea, *the* big statement, I stopped and just started building. Building what she had built time and time again. What the ancients had made. A permanent home, *the* heart of the matter. Something that held the past, present and future. A place where long after you had left this life, your offspring could be protected and nurtured. A place where they could remember and honour you. A container of love.

On a weekend visit to my brother, who now lives in Leadhills, I found the perfect place. Countless streams peppered with whitened grey stones. They were long, flat and softly rounded. Quickly placing some on the grass, one could instantly see the curvature of a broch. I gathered as many as I could that day and took them into the Project. Maybe it was because I raved about Leadhills so much or they liked the stones, but it was decided that we would organise a trip; the dual purpose being a nice day out for the clientele and the collection of enough stones to finish the Stone Project. The reason I had sold the idea so well was this – I had seen a different kind of beauty in the Southern Uplands of Scotland. Not the twee, manicured, tourist hot spots we all know so well. This was a scarred landscape, a place that had sustained pain, where a raw honesty peered back at you from those stone-strafed hills.

During this time Christine had become like a menopausal adolescent. She had dyed her hair blonde; it suited her and I think she knew it. Well, it had worked for Ann Widdecombe so it certainly had done wonders for Christine. She missed a couple of sessions and I was told she had been a very naughty girl and had been confined to Jericho House. The reason for the confinement was this – she had jumped into a taxi in Chambers Street and asked to be taken to Gorebridge. Request granted, she was then taken to Gorebridge police station when she couldn't pay the fare. I was so annoyed at hearing this, not at her but at that pure prick of a taxi driver. In a just world, he should have been marched into a cell by four policemen. And before they proceeded to kick utter fuck out of him they should have asked this question: 'A woman looking like her gets into your cab, can of beer and cigarette in one hand and a trinket of super lagers dangling from the other. She says "Gorebridge" and you don't think to check if she's got the money? Did you think she'd cashed her Giro? Think you'd got a daftie, an easy touch?' Aaargh! But it's not a just world. So she was detained and he went on his merry way back home. No doubt rehearsing the story he was going to tell his equally arsehole taxi-driver mates at the various ranks throughout the city.

Here's the difference between him and her. She was probably genuinely pleased at how nice the cop shop was compared to previous visits in her youth. I hoped when the police eventually drove her home that they took the scenic route; a wee trip down memory lane. Good on her, despite the punishment she had received, to see Gorebridge again.

On her return to the Project someone told her of the proposed trip to Leadhills. She was desperate to go. I wanted her to go. Some members of staff pointed out that maybe the trip would too much for her; that maybe she might not cope. I knew the script, but I can't be too critical; if she had an accident (maybe several), I would not be the one who had to change her. It was the phrase 'might not cope' that bugged me. When I thought of all the abuse she had suffered, all the rotten things that had happened to her and how none of that had changed the goodness in her. Coped, she had fucking excelled. It all became academic really. The trip had been pencilled in for 29 April. Sometime on 6 March, Christine died; she was 56.

I was told the news on my return from Glasgow. It was the way they told me that hit home. Lucy said she had some bad news to tell me – pausing, before saying she knew I was really close to her. Those words made me realise how her life had touched mine.

The only information certain at the moment was that she was dead. I know it was not only my head that was putting two and two together and coming up with 224. All that was in my head was that I just hoped nobody had hurt her, that nothing bad had happened. Later that day we found out that nothing bad had happened. She had gone to bed and sometime during the night she had just stopped. Stopped, that was it. That yellow-brick motorway to Gorebridge would never reach completion.

The funeral was brilliant – that's the only word for it. The chapel at Morton Hall was full. Numerous minibuses had brought people from the hostels of the city; there were drunks, and people struggling not to be drunk; the city's un-fortunates, fortunate enough to have known her. There were lots of carers. Church people and musicians gathered there for a celebration. The hymns had been picked by her. Reggae hymns, whose sweet words complemented the music. During the minister's eulogy, a drunk guy stood up determined to have his say. The minister let him have his say. 'A've known Christine for 20 years and she never bothered naebody, never bothered naebody, and, and she never had a bad word to be said about anybody.' With that he slumped back on his chair. It was as if the power of his truth had totally exhausted him. The minister finished his heartfelt tribute and Christine left this world to the raucous singing of 'Oh, When the Saints Go Marching In'. As I left the chapel I saw her father. This was the only tinge of sadness that I felt. If life had been hard on her it had been just as hard on him. Her soul now freed from its interment in that big ungainly frame would be caressing and enhancing the golden fields of Gorebridge. And unlike Heathcliff's Cathy, her soul would wait silently and patiently for the return of her three babies.

Some Secret, Some Shame

Tom Kyle

The First Minister is fond of referring to sectarianism as 'Scotland's secret shame'. In the Scotland where I grew up it was no secret – and it certainly wasn't regarded as being shameful.

The product of a mixed marriage, I have never really quite understood how my mother and father were ever together in the first place. She was a Glasgow Protestant; he a Catholic of Irish descent. Staunch is a word scarcely robust enough to describe my mother's Protestantism. I heard her once being asked if she was a Christian. 'No,' she replied, 'I'm a Protestant.'

Born in Bridgeton in the days of open gang warfare between the Billy Boys and the Norman Conks, mother has always known where she stood vis-à-vis religion.

As a young woman, she went out to buy an evening paper one Friday in July. She didn't reappear for days, having hooked up with a flute band on its way to Belfast for the Orange Walk. This may have been how she met Sam the Sailor, a semi-mythical Shankill man to whom she subsequently considered herself engaged. Sam's commitment appears to have been less wholehearted. After a number of missives to various corners of the oceans had gone unanswered, mother wrote to his captain. It seems she fully expected Sam to be clapped in irons until he could be brought back to the Broom-ielaw and her.

His inconstancy did little to shake mother's faith. Ecclesiastically, had she ever thought in such terms, she would have been on the Cameronian wing of the Covenanters. Though regarded in an almost romantic light nowadays, the Covenanters were intent on imposing their religion on the rest of humanity, with little regard for the lives of others or themselves. They were the al-Qaeda of their day. Mother would have fitted in perfectly.

Somehow, then, she met my father, exactly how, when or why I have never known. My memories are fragmentary; my vagueness inevitable. Mother spoke of the whole business very, very rarely and never in any detail; my father I never knew. One of the few things I ever learned about their relationship was revealed in a slanging match with mother when I was about 18 and extremely drunk. The memory is a little indistinct, but I think I had probably goaded her about shagging Catholics when she hated them so much. Just as well she had, I said, or I wouldn't have been here. She told me it was the first time they had ever had sex – I'm not sure if it was the first time she had ever had sex – and that she had been paying for it ever since.

So there she was, pregnant and unwed. In those days, there was only one thing to be done. However unsavoury the idea, she was going to have to marry a Catholic. It was not a big wedding. I'm not even sure any of mother's family were there. The dirty deed done – the wedding, that is, not my less than immaculate conception – they set up home in Scotstoun. When I was, I think, one-and-a-bit, my father sneaked me off to be baptised into the Church of Rome at St Paul's in Partick. Although scarcely a voluntary participant, I have some vague half-memory of going along with the idea. I think it was the little silver St Christopher medal that swung it for me.

I think it was the little silver St Christopher medal that swung it for mother as well. She pulled it from my neck, threw it away, put me in my pram and walked the three miles to her mother, whose proudest possession was a painting of King Billy on his big white horse, crossing the Boyne. The walk, pushing me and the pram mostly uphill, was no hardship for mother; she had done it every day since I had arrived home from the maternity hospital.

That day, she never went back. It was, I think, the second last time I ever saw my father. The last would have been when I was five or six. It was a December night, shortly before Christmas, when suddenly there was a knock at the door. Mother went to answer it. I followed her to the top of the stairs and peeked surreptitiously round the corner to see who could be calling at such a late and unexpected hour. When mother opened the door, I could just make out the figure of a man carrying a brightly wrapped package. Not a word was spoken. Mother simply slapped the man across the face and slammed the door. It was, I believe, my father with a Christmas present for me.

Mother's view of her separation from my father – they never, so far as I know, divorced – was simple and direct. As was her view of most things. 'So long as I don't take a penny piece from him,' she never tired of telling me, 'he cannae see you.' A penny piece obviously included Christmas presents. I doubt her analysis of parental right-of-access would have carried much legal weight, even at the time, but it was to be her deeply held mantra throughout my early years. Along with telling me that my father was the worst man who had ever walked God's Earth.

It must have been a great disappointment to mother that her attempted indoctrination of me into the Protestant faith fell on stony ground. When the time came for my own early forays into the unknown world of sexual shenanigans, it was perhaps inevitable that my first serious girlfriend would turn out to be a Catholic. It wasn't planned as any sort of rebellion; it just happened that way.

Mother's reaction was as vile as it was predictable. 'A brazen little Catholic bitch,' was her considered opinion, 'with the map of Ireland written all over her face.' When I much later came to be married, my wife-to-be was not pregnant. Nor was she a Catholic. Not that the Anglican Church ranked much higher in my mother's estimation, 'Church of England? No' a kick in the arse aff bein' a Pape.'

What mother would have made of my own son being baptised a Catholic, albeit in a hospital ward on a makeshift altar fashioned from a trolley, I can easily imagine. I myself have never been a practising Catholic, but it seemed the right thing to do in the face of major open-heart surgery at ten days old. On the morning of our son's operation, my wife and I went to pray at the very church where my own father had had me baptised all those years previously. Again, it just seemed the right thing to do. Our son survived. I like to think my father would have liked that.

I almost met him when I was at university. By chance, one of my contemporaries was a cousin. My father was her favourite uncle. I never did meet him, though. I probably would have done, had my cousin not left university suddenly. We lost touch and I never saw her again – or him.

I think he's dead now. Another cousin, on my mother's side, saw a death notice in a newspaper and seemed to think it was him. It likely was. Mother's still alive, though. She's 80 now and in a care home with Alzheimer's. She doesn't remember who I am – but she hasn't forgotten how to be a bigot.

Nor, sadly, have so many Scots who profess to hold religion dear. But they do have a sense of their place, these defenders of the faithless; a sense of their place as God's chosen people. Whatever these people, chosen or otherwise, are – a joke, a nuisance, a danger, take your pick – one thing they are not is the 'tiny minority' beloved of politicians and soccer pundits. Look at God's storm troopers in the front line at any Old Firm game. It may only be a minority (though I'm unconvinced it's that tiny) who actually attack those of the opposite persuasion – and violence is far from 'casual' when you're on the receiving end of it – but there is huge underlying tacit support from the thousands upon thousands who scream the songs and chants of hatred. And anyone who thinks it's only a 'tiny minority' who do that at Rangers-Celtic games has clearly never been to one.

I have only ever had a sense of being out of place in the place where I was raised. If my own family history, however incomplete, has taught me anything, however, it is that a problem so deep-seated as sectarianism in Scotland won't be solved by a soundbite. That's no secret, First Minister, though it is a shame.

The Road to Tynecastle Park

Kenny Gilchrist

The maroon double-decker bus edged its way along the road, trundling behind the rest of the Saturday afternoon traffic. It was August, Festival time in the capital city, but this type of entertainment isn't advertised in some fancy Festival guide handed out to any old tourist on the Royal Mile.

The bus ambled on to Dalry Road in between the canyons of the soot-sprinkled tenements. This used to be one of the working-class areas of Edinburgh but it is now being slowly gentrified with upmarket restaurants. Internet cafés and delicatessens were spreading along Gorgie Road like crocuses popping up in spring hoping to bloom with the new money that is being tied up in the new building developments in the area. From his upper level seat on the bus, he could see the large floodlights of Tynecastle Park zoom into view, like giant chessmen crouched at the four corners of the pitch. It was a hot summer's afternoon and the bus was packed full. People were standing in the aisles, grappling with the plastic straps that were there to help them keep their balance and stop them from falling onto the seated passengers. He could somehow sense electricity in the air of anticipation crackling between the passengers. The chattering and laughter before the game – 'the banter' it is called in some parts – a feel-good factor that verified he had made the right decision in getting the bus along instead of a taxi. Just before the railway bridge, which carries the trains west towards Glasgow, the bus came to a halt and, like soldiers marching off to war, the majority of the passengers sprung up out of their seats without being told and disembarked. They dissolved quickly into the throng of people making their way along the Gorgie Road towards Tynecastle Stadium and the new football revolution which the club is undergoing.

This Saturday ritual in some shape or form has been going on since 1881 when people came by horse and cart, tram or train, when there was an actual train station on Gorgie Road and the steam trains used to stop. The fashions might have changed through history but, like death and taxes, the football club has been a constant part of the community and the city of Edinburgh since 1874. This was the club he had supported from when he was a small boy. The club that his faither had supported and his faither's uncles had supported. He could remember the shed in the corner of the ground where the Gorgie boot boys used to congregate to chant and sing obscenities to the opposing team's players or fans; the old-fashioned floodlight pylons embedded deep into the concrete terracing and the whiff of hops and yeast that used to hang over the ground. Now, under the football sanitation of the early 90s, it was made all-seated, all shiny plastic and the brewery was sold off for more upmarket housing. All this has gone like autumnal leaves decaying on the ground.

Walking past the Tynecastle Arms pub, an old-fashioned drinking establishment still serving 80 shilling beer on draught and scotch pies to its clientele, he passed under the sporting pub sign showing a goalkeeper bravely diving at a forward's feet. This was McLeod Street, the entrance to the famous maroon-clad stadium. He put his hand into his front left pocket and brought out two pound coins. A small huddle of people were around a man selling the programmes for the big match. It was a bit like a rugby scrum as hands thrust out money from various angles in exchange for a small paper pamphlet. He flipped his copy round to the back, slowly digesting the names of the players who would be playing in the maroon jersey that afternoon. Ah good – he said to himself – our star striker is fit to play and back in the team.

He put his hand into his back right pocket and brought out a folded piece of paper which he unravelled. Glancing at it, he registered that this was in fact his match ticket for the game and he got into line as a snake of people queued to go through the old metal turnstile. Soon it would be his turn to hand over his ticket and hear the click, click, click of the turnstile.

Ullapool

Nuala Ní Chonchúir

I arrived in Ullapool, a fishing village cosily settled on the shores of Loch Broom, the day after sitting my final exams at Trinity College Dublin. Hungry for a change and eager for work that didn't involve study, I was there to take up a much-coveted summer job at a hotel. The 'hotel' turned out to be a lot more than that name suggests: it was a cultural centre, bookshop, art gallery, music venue, and it had a fine restaurant, among many other things. In Ireland, jobs were scarce – these were the pre-Celtic Tiger years of the early 90s – and I was grateful for the work. The weather was summery and Tracey – my new friend from Glasgow – and I complained at the un-Highlandish nature of the hot sun: we wanted turbulent mists and brooding skies. The heat lasted two weeks and didn't return for the duration of my stay.

I had studied Scots Gàidhlig as part of my degree in the Irish language and, on a scholarship to a summer course at Sabhal Mòr Ostaig on Skye, had fallen in love with the Highlands. It wasn't just the language, or the angular vastness of the mountains, or the sight of the odd strip-limbed tree stalking the landscape – though these things were beautiful – it was, like most places we become attached to, as much about the people as the setting. I loved the welcome I received, the kinship shown to me as a fellow Celt – we were all a part of the same clan. As my father would have it, both our countries had at various times been 'swallowed up in the belly of another nation'. Some of the other things that sang to me were the lilt of the accents, the passion for political discussion among people my own age, the almost American 'can-do' attitude to life, and the ironic sense of humour. After Skye, I had planned a longer return trip to Scotland.

I settled quickly into life in the hotel in Ullapool, enjoying long working days in the restaurant and fun nights with my workmates, who came from the Antipodes, Edinburgh, England, Glasgow, and the village itself. I became a member of Greenpeace; travelled further north on my days off to see the mass of Stac Pollaidh, Thurso, the poet Rob Donn's burial place at Durness, Smoo Cave. I made friends, took lovers, entertained notions of being a writer.

A summer of ferry trips, porpoise and seal-watching in the sea loch and beyond, disco-dancing with welly-booted fishermen – who also worked behind bars, or were postmen or chefs – quickly turned to autumn, and then winter. My graduation from Trinity sent me home to Ireland for a week in November, but I happily returned to Ullapool. And then I stayed on and on, not able to break free from the draw of the place and its people.

The hotel proprietors ran a bakery/café/wholefood shop on Shore Street and I went to work there, opening the bakery shop in the mornings. I would shuffle out of bed in the dark and skitter along by the pier, listening to the musical slap of ropes against masts and watching oily-headed seals bobbing nosily in the harbour. The salt-fish smell of the sea filled my mouth.

Cakes for the bakery shop were sent down fresh each morning from the hotel kitchen – fat scones, chewy meringues, bakewells, strawberry tarts. The bulk of the bread was collected from far-off Inverness by John, a local man, and he brought it to me to lay out on my shelves, while dawn found its way in from the sea. John's delivery was late only twice. Once he had hit a stag in the dim morning light on the road back to Ullapool. The stag, he said, was gashed and bloodied and took off into the trees, but both he and the small white van were badly shaken by the time they pulled up at my door. The second time John arrived late, he had been caught in a snowstorm and got stuck in a drift on the long road back. I had been told it never snowed in the village, or at least that the snow never 'lay'. But I got up that January morning to a sparkling coverlet, that was as white as the icing on the creamy dream-rings that sold out first thing every morning in the bakery. I had no bread to offer to the hungry Ullapudlians until late that wintry afternoon, but the snowfall had even my grumbliest customers chatty and smiling.

Ullapool to me was friendship, difference, music, eye-opening people and events, great wholesome food, earnest chatter and light fun. It was Loch Broom through the seasons – wild, flat calm, inviting, gorgeous. It was an enthusiastic English touring company's *Hamlet*, my first reading of *The Lonely Passion of Judith Hearne*, and a wood-lined dormer house my flatmates and I not-so-fondly christened 'the Fridge'. It was buying stinky cigarettes and Matrushka dolls from a Klondiker, and happily paying over the odds, because I reckoned he needed the money more than I did. It was a contented Christmas away from home.

I left Ullapool in the spring and flew home to Ireland, holding a legacy inside me that I hadn't planned for – new life.

And so, that Highland fishing village with its peculiar Nordic name, a place of happy times and valuable learning, gifted me something more tangible than memories to remember it by – it gave me my son.

In the Land of Pines

John Fowler

Some years ago I set out on a journey of discovery, hoping to find traces of the Old Caledonian Forest which, according to legend, covered most of Scotland in the distant past, but which has since degenerated into a random patchwork of elderly trees in otherwise bare Highland glens. Of course, I knew that this forest – or Great Wood of Caledon, to give it an even grander title – is now generally dismissed as mythical, the product of 19th century romanticism (which could be said of Caledonia itself – the 'Caledonia, stern and wild' of Scott's imagining). But the idea of a great and widespread primeval forest, whether you call it old Caledonian or not, is seductive, and indeed accords pretty well with reality. Woodland advanced and declined in prehistoric times according to fluctuations in climate, and at its greatest extent in Scotland, during long periods of warmth thousands of years ago, woodland spread upwards almost to the mountain tops. Colder weather, the insidious build-up of peat bogs, and finally deforestation and exploitation by mankind led to its disastrous decline.

It's a common belief that the trees in this supposed Caledonian forest were predominantly pines of the species *Pinus sylvestris*, which we are content to call Scots pine though it grows widely all across northern Europe, right to the edge of the Bering Sea. Pine was not alone. Broadleaf trees such as oak – dominant in the western parts – hazel, birch and ash were also swift to recolonise Scotland after the Ice Age glaciers melted, leaving the landscape bare. Yet Scots pine is uniquely our iconic tree.

I set out on my winter journey with a book in hand – *The Native Pinewoods of Scotland* by H.M. Steven, one-time Professor of Forestry at Aberdeen University, and his research assistant Alan (better known as Jock, though he was an Englishman) Carlisle. The young Carlisle spent several energetic and adventurous years in the 1950s tramping remote parts of Scotland in fair weather and foul in a quest to identify remnants of the original pine forest; trees, as he wrote, which had 'descended from one generation to another by natural means' from the earliest progenitors and were thus lineal descendants of the forest pioneers. Thirty-five sites were listed by Steven and Carlisle, though others, mainly mere scraps of woodland in reclusive gorges or distant corries, have since been added.

My first stop that winter's day in 1993 was in the relatively accessible Black Wood of Rannoch, by the loch of the same name, reached from the A9 by a narrow winding road which that morning was reported closed to traffic. There had been fierce gales of wind and driving snow, and just past the village of Tummel Bridge the river had broken its banks and submerged the carriageway. I nervously ploughed through the flood, trusting to follow a car driven by a local.

Like many relic pinewoods, the old trees of the Black Wood are hedged in by later plantations. Only the core is old forest, and even that is not what Americans would term 'old growth', meaning pristine, unravished natural woodland. There is a long history of timber extraction. People have worked the

Black Wood for profit over centuries, and you still find narrow ditches overgrown with vegetation which once were channels dug to transport logs down to the lochside sawmill.

On and around this spot, pines have flourished for millennia, ebbing and flowing according to their nature and the condition of soil and climate. The growing Scots pine seeks light and does not tolerate shade, unhappy under a dark canopy of foliage. In that sense a pinewood is unstable, ever moving beyond its bounds and then reoccupying lost ground when old trees fall and create new space. It tiptoes about in (very) slow motion.

That day the hills were white, blotched on the lower slopes by the dark crowns of outlying pine trees. Within the wood, dollops of snow slid from overhanging branches and underfoot I squelched through damp vegetation – humps of heather and many-coloured mosses – and skirted half-hidden pools and small streams.

Here in the Black Wood the old Caledonian pines can be seen at their grandest. I passed a huge specimen, big as a house, standing proud on a knoll. Such rugged ancients, stout in the stem, are plated with ridged and creviced bark, home to many lichens. Their heavy branches twist and turn, rising skywards or bending almost to the ground as if in a gigantic wrestling match with unseen powers. The orange tint of the upper branches glows like fire in slanting sunlight.

On this occasion the combination of a heavy mantle of snow and gusting wind had brought many boughs crashing to the ground. Out on the hillside I found the wreckage of one great tree newly felled by the storm. It had snapped some ten feet from the base and the blasted trunk lay like a beached monster on the slope above. From the shattered heartwood the heavy fragrance of pine resin filled the air. A year later I found the ruin in a changed state. The vivid living timber had weathered to dull grey, bright pinpoints of fungus mottled a rain-darkened patch where the bark had peeled off, the once-green needles had turned brown, and the pine perfume had long since vaporised away. Corruption had set in; the tree was dead, though in its decay it gave sustenance to a multitude of lesser forms of life.

I spent several years, off and on, seeking out relic pine-woods. The frequently bad weather was no bar; in fact it added to the exhilaration. There is a particular exaltation in walking among trees when the boughs are swaying and the wind is roaring in the tops. I have stopped the car beside the Atlantic shore at Shieldaig, where the most westerly group of ancient pines crowd along terraced rocks, and when I opened the door a flurry of snow blew in. I have perched on a rock in what is reputedly the highest significant stand of ancient pines, high above Loch an Eilein in Strathspey, clutching a soggy sandwich in chilled fingers as snowflakes whirled in the wind. At that elevation, the trees are small and gnarled; higher still they struggle against the elements as isolated, stunted bushes. One misty day I found a mere wisp of needle-tufts wedged in a mossy rock, just a few inches of growth flattened by the winds, so small that I could have scraped it out with my boot. But it was a Scots pine nevertheless, and probably years in the growing.

There are marvellous trees in Strathspey and in the upper glens of Deeside. Not far north of Loch Morlich in Glenmore, where holiday crowds picnic on the shore, a well-trodden track leads through the Pass of Ryvoan. The hills close round a small circle of water, An Lochan Uaine, the green loch. Above it, there is a scattering of pine trees on a steep scree slope. Every so often a senescent tree loses its grip and is torn from its roots by a gale, to slide down into the water where, below the surface, the remains of previous victims can be seen lodged on the murky bottom.

The green loch isn't difficult to reach. Hill-walkers pass by in droves, since it's on the direct route to Cairngorm peaks. Countless holiday strollers make their way there. A good track leads out of Glenmore to Abernethy, another historic pinewood, on a stretch of moorland where I doubt if you are ever out of sight of a pine tree – here a lone specimen, there a clustered few – the last survivors of what was once unbroken forest. Here, too, can be found lochans secreted in heathery hollows which once formed a system of pounds and dams, where a head of water could be built up to feed into the River Spey, so that logs could be sent tumbling downstream to the coast. Such timber floating was carried on throughout the Highland pinewoods from the 18th century or earlier until well into the 1900s. During two world wars the old forests suffered heavy fellings, mainly by contingents of loggers brought over from Canada and Newfoundland.

Far up in the recesses of Glen Cannich, north of the Great Glen, some of the old pine trees still bear scars where the wartime fellers made initial axe cuts but for some reason failed to finish the job with crosscut saws. Who knows why they paused? Perhaps peace was declared between breakfast and dinnertime; they laid down their tools and never came back.

Glen Cannich is one of three neighbouring glens where substantial remnant forests survive – indeed, thrive – now that care is being taken to preserve the trees and to encourage regeneration. All three are widely different in character. Glen Strathfarrar, the longest and loneliest, leads into some of the most inhospitable mountain territory in the country. Far up the glen, swathes and drifts of the noblest old trees enliven the rocky hillsides. Cannich and Strathfarrar are seldom visited (the road up Glen Strathfarrar is private, and entry for vehicles is limited), but Glen Affric is popular with sightseers, particularly admired in autumn when the dark-green pine tree crowns contrast with the golden flush of birch. Beyond the last car park, a track winds alongside a rushing river among scattered ancient pines, and as you climb above Loch Affric you may look down, in calm weather, on a pattern of hillside and old forest perfectly mirrored in the water. With a good deal more effort you will reach, some miles beyond, a denuded landscape in which the bare bones of a long-lost pinewood are embedded in the valley flats – star-clusters of whitened root systems which have been preserved for an era in the oozy peat.

You don't have to travel so far to see relic pinewoods. Some can be glimpsed from the road. A little north of Loch Lomond, nearing Crianlarich, are a hundred or so gaunt survivors, their numbers sadly reduced by the sheep which until recently roamed freely among them. Sheep, gobblers of all green shoots, are, along with deer, the arch destroyers of woodland. Further north, as the same A82 road approaches Tyndrum, with Ben Lui in sight, domed old pines can be spotted on the rough ground under the mountains, or, a little further on, before the road climbs steeply towards Rannoch Moor, spreading around Loch Tulla.

It's probably those less accessible pinewoods that I find most attractive. Usually they involve an arduous hike on mountain tracks or even where no track exists and a way has to be forced through knee-high heather and across brown burns. In the upper reaches of Rhidorroch in Wester Ross there is a rack of overhanging cliff and a waste of tumbled boulders where stunted pine trees manage to survive, while, high above, a few airy siblings, spindle-shanked and thinly foliaged, caper on the skyline.

I treasure another memory. From Glen Shiel a rough road leads southwards into wild country before coming to an abrupt halt at Loch Loyne. Nowadays it's a road to nowhere, although before the loch was dammed for hydro power and the rising waters cut it off, it was a road to the Isles. Masonry culverts and embankments are reminders of its past. It's no longer a public way and a locked gate bars entry to unauthorised vehicles. But if you penetrate the further reaches you may see, if you know where to look, a distant scrap of woodland under a craggy spur. In this case woodland is somewhat of a misnomer, a few scattered trees that appear to be in terminal decline.

But they have a special claim to attention. A few years ago a researcher extracted core samples and when the growth rings on the cores were counted some trees proved to be over 500 years old. They were growing when Mary Queen of Scots came to the throne. These are the oldest trees of their kind, so far as we know – until then it was believed that the age limit of native pine trees grown on Scottish soil was 400 years at best. So there is a direct link, of not so many generations, between today's gaunt veterans in Glen Loyne and the first trees that took root there after the ice withdrew.

Three of us visited Glen Loyne on that occasion. One laid his hands reverentially on the most ancient pine tree of all, pressed his forehead to the rough bark, and closed his eyes. For him, it was a spiritual moment. Even I, less of a mystic than he, sensed that we stood on hallowed ground.

A Man in Assynt

Brian McCabe

Going to Assynt feels like going home, even if you've never been there before. At least it did to me, when I spent a week there with my family recently. I'd been as far north as Assynt a few times before, but without this same sense of arriving in a place I already knew and loved.

I had been to Wick to give a poetry reading, when the land was icebound one February, and it had seemed like another planet. I was with a Gaelic poet and we had ended up listening to the proprietor of the Indian restaurant telling us how, when he first opened, the local police came with sniffer dogs during the night to search his premises. They took away his cumin and his turmeric for analysis.

I had been to Lewis, in the hippyish 70s, but that bare island had felt bleak and alien – a feeling reinforced by going along to the local church one Sunday with my beflowered and beflared friends, where the Free Church minister took the opportunity to point the finger at us for most of the ills of the modern world.

The landscape of Assynt is imposing, even majestic, but at the same time deeply reassuring. It is gloriously empty, but lush with heather, teeming with rivers and waterfalls, and bejewelled by hundreds of lochs. The mountains are distinct individuals, standing in their own space like actors on a stage, but unless you plod a few miles over the boggy peat moors to climb them, they remain as characters in a distant, primordial drama – visually compelling and, what is better, requiring no audience participation if you don't feel up for it.

We stayed at Clashnessie, a hamlet on the coast a few miles north of Lochinver. Part of the feeling of homecoming undoubtedly came from the homeliness of the cottage we had rented. There was the same carpet from the home of my childhood, surrounded by the same 'parquet-wood' style of linoleum. There were electric blankets, a carpet-sweeper in the cupboard under the stairs and those wee plates on the wall decorated with fronds and ferns, barely big enough to hold a biscuit. Not that they had ever been required to hold a biscuit.

The cottage was perched above the beach – a clean, crescent of pinkish sand looking out on the Minch. On a clear night it is possible to see the lights of Stornoway and according to a local saying, if you can see them, it's going to rain and if you can't, it is raining.

What became clearer to me as the days passed was that I felt recognition and fondness for this landscape because I had read about it so much in Norman MacCaig's poetry. Here I was, driving around the winding, single-track roads – 'You're an acrobat with a bulrushy spine / looping in air' – and walking from one small loch to another – 'Dandling lilies and talking sleepily / And standing huge mountains on their heads' – and looking at mountains – 'Suilven and Cul Mor, my / mountains of mountains / looming and pachydermatous in the thin light / of a clear half moon' – but I had the very peculiar feeling that really I was just wandering about inside Norman MacCaig's head.

He came here with his family every summer for over 40 years, staying a couple of miles out of Lochinver at the Bay of Achmelvich. He walked, climbed and fished all over Assynt, and he and his wife Isabel were much loved by people in the community. Though I had known about MacCaig's 'other home' in Assynt, somehow being there brought home to me just how important the place was to him, and how extensively it featured in his poetry. MacCaig made it his own poetic territory, the landscape in which he viewed nature and humanity, and we can almost hear his decision to do so in 'Climbing Suilven':

> *Parishes dwindle. But my parish is*
> *This stone, that tuft, this stone*
> *And the cramped quarters of my flesh and bone.*

In a sense, MacCaig has given the stones and tufts of Assynt a meaning they didn't have before, and that is the business of poetry. Almost every bird and rock and stream I saw seemed to suggest another line from MacCaig. On a walk to see the waterfall at Clashnessie, I urged my daughter to feel the thick, soft moss on a stone and she said it felt like a cushion. Yes, and MacCaig thought so too, though he didn't leave it at that:

> *… The mosses on the wall*
> *Plump their fat cushions up. They smell of wells,*
> *Of under bridges and of spoons. They move*
> *more quiveringly than the dazed rims of bells.*

> From 'By Achmelvich Bridge'

It's remarkable how much accurate observation he can pack into four short lines, and there is an immediate recognition that mosses do indeed smell of wells, undersides of bridges and spoons, but what astonishes is the bold connection he draws between the movement of moss and 'the dazed rims of bells'. That sort of leap of the imagination takes genius.

MacCaig was not content to write descriptive poems about the landscape, but was very much aware of the people and how they live, and was able to describe their work with great clarity, as in 'Sheep Dipping, Achmelvich':

> *...When*
> *John chucks the ewe in, she splays up two wings*
> *That beat once and are water once again.*

Water is said to be one of the most difficult things to paint, let alone paint with words, and its prevalence in Assynt provided MacCaig with a constant challenge. In his poetry it becomes ropes, nets, coins, wings, antlers, hands, and it speaks with a voice which sounds garrulously human.

He is always looking for and finding such connections between the natural world and the human one. Sometimes he does this in order to demonstrate the inability of the human mind to do anything but see things in its own terms. In 'Humanism' he describes the formation of Glen Canisp as a battle between glacier and rock, then says:

> *... what*
> *arrogance, not to allow*
> *a glacier to be a glacier –*
> *to humanise into a metaphor*
> *that long slither of ice – that was no more*
> *a beaten army than it was a horde*
> *of Cinderellas ...*

And he concludes by respecting the glacier because, when it absorbs a man, it 'preserves his image intact'.

After a few days exploring Assynt and musing on Mac-Caig's poetry, I decided to visit Norman MacAskill, a very good friend of Norman and Isabel's and, I had heard, a fisherman of some note himself. (One local story has it that he once caught the largest salmon ever found in the area, but couldn't record the catch because it was poached.) I left my wife and children on the beach at Clashnessie and drove to Lochinver, a little nervous about going to see a man I had never met before. By the time I'd reached Clachtoll, it was pouring with rain, and I wondered if I should turn back to run my family to the cottage. No, I thought, they'll be back inside by now. When Mr MacAskill opened his door, he said to me, 'Go and phone your wife to apologise for locking her out!' I had locked the door – that strange, city habit – and had driven off with the key in my pocket. As it happened, a neighbour had seen my family out in the rain and had come to their aid, providing them not only with Mr MacAskill's phone number, but also tea and biscuits, books for the children to read, and warmth and shelter until my return.

MacAskill seemed tickled by all this. He gave me a dram and told me about MacCaig's times in Assynt. For many years, to begin with, people didn't know he was a poet – or if they did, didn't bother too much about it. It was the man they took to. I talked about his effect on me and other writers of my generation in Scotland, and that too was not a question of literary influence – it was also the man who embodied something, a questioning, clear-minded spirit which cut through cant and pretentiousness.

Naturally, we came around to discussing MacCaig's long poem 'A Man in Assynt', which people from Assynt think most highly of. The poem is a sustained paean to the place, culminating in an eloquent plea for its survival

that sad withdrawal of people, may, too,
reverse itself and flood
the bays and the sheltered glens
with new generations replenishing the land
with its richest of riches and coming, at last,
into their own again.

To some extent this replenishing has taken place, the crofters having won the right to own their land. MacCaig's poem, published in the local newspaper at the time of the crofters' campaign, years after it was written, became instrumental in this change. Assynt gave MacCaig a world in which he was able to grow and mature as a poet, but he also gave something valuable to it – a poetry worthy of its primal beauty – and that has had a practical, commercial effect. Assynt needs people, and no glossy brochure could have served the place so well as MacCaig's poems.

Infinite Scotland

Paul Johnston

Stone and sea, rain and fleeting sun have always been here. Birds, too, keening and swooping over doomed wild creatures – bears, aurochs, wolves. Scotland-before-Scotland was a crumpled giant of rock stretching vainly westwards towards its lost children, the islands. Our human ancestors were late arrivals, but soon their imprint was clear. The land was changed forever.

How to write about this place, this nation, this knot of dualities and contradictions, in a fresh way? Surely it has all been said before by superior minds and pens. The great makars and novelists – Burns, Scott, Stevenson, Muir, Grassic Gibbon, MacCaig, the whole native pantheon – had close links with the land. It was the shaper of their language and thought, their characters and tales. And, in turn, they transformed Scotland by wrestling with it. They buried their hands in its soil and peat, then washed them in its lochs, salt and sweet, and in its icy tarns. What is there left to say?

Nae worries. Everyone has their own story to tell, and this is mine.

I was born in Edinburgh to Scots parents, whose parents were also 'pure' Scots. There has been muttered talk of earlier immigrants from the Baltic States. Maybe I will trace that line some time – we're all Europeans now. I went to primary school in a small village in Berwickshire. Our house was isolated, a white building originally used by Irish farm workers. I remember the warm reek of the hen coop, the scurry of weasels up the track, the slapping sting of the tawse. My friends were farmers' sons. We built castles out of hay bales, used the old pillbox on the moor as a base for military operations, paid no attention to the sheep and cows. Or to the land. But, unnoticed, it sank into us and gradually made its presence felt. My schoolmates are farmers themselves now. But I was uprooted, willingly.

I went to school in Edinburgh because – get this – I'd decided that I wanted to learn ancient Greek. There was a copy of the Penguin translation of Homer's *Odyssey* in the house and I found it irresistible – a brave and cunning hero, a succession of monsters, gruesome violence, and a happy ending. What more could a boy want? By comparison, the Scottish history we did at school was gloomy and dispiriting. After the scarcely credible victory at Bannockburn, it was a sorry concatenation of clan feuding, the wrenching horror of Flodden and Culloden, and feeble monarchs. Where was the hope in that?

So I got stuck into the ancient world. I remember opening my Greek primer in the first lesson and examining the map of the Aegean. It never occurred to me that the scattered islands and wave-lashed coasts were the mirror-image of my own country's topology. I suppose growing up is all about escape and discovering new worlds. From early on I'd been fascinated by the sense of a different place. I spent six months in Greece before university. The bare mountains and dusty terraces were completely different from my homeland's heather-covered slopes and multiple shades of green, but they were closer to my heart.

I continued studying the classics at university, but something had changed. I now found myself more in tune with contemporary Greece – the language, the spirit of the people, the seductive glories of the landscape. After changing my degree, I concentrated on modern Greek novelists and poets, eventually doing postgraduate studies in comparative literature. I even wrote a dissertation on the fictional landscapes of, not Scottish writers, but D.H. Lawrence and the Greek Stratis Myrivilis. I was a specialist in the sense of place, but for me Scotland had become a utopia in the original sense of the word – somewhere that didn't exist. Depression caused by the failed devolution vote in 1979 was definitely part of the problem. Whatever you think of Greece, it had managed to achieve independence. It had even voted out its monarchy. Where did that leave the Scots?

I still came home regularly, to Edinburgh and to Berwickshire. I still ventured into the wilder Scotland, revisiting the peaks we had scaled in the school hill-walking club – Schiehallion, Ben Lawers, the Cobbler, Ben Vorlich. Those Munros seemed insignificant after the soaring masses of Parnassus and Olympus, but they moved me all the same. The soft cladding of moss and bracken, burns that quenched your thirst even in high summer, the ridges that stepped away to hidden glens – there was an old love stirring.

But I continued to spend much of my time in Greece, having moved to a small island to start writing. This turned out to be a flawed plan. Although I had the time to concentrate, as well as peace and quiet (the house was called 'Serenity'), I found myself very cut off from the outside world. In a word, isolated. I often thought of my idol Lawrence's story 'The Man Who Loved Islands', in which a character apparently based on Compton Mackenzie moves to ever smaller and hostile isles in pursuit of a perverted kind of solitude. Then I remembered another of my favourite writers, Robert Louis Stevenson. He had written about Scotland from Western Samoa, the enormous distance giving him a degree of objectivity. He was also nostalgic for the old country. Aware of the etymology (nostalgia = the pain for return), I began to realise that using my hitherto scarcely noticed homesickness might actually help my writing.

And it did. I had been trying to construct literary novels about Gallipoli, the Falklands, the Trojan War, the long-lasting effects of a student production of 'The Tempest', Greek islands, and tragic love affairs. I took stock. There were three salient characteristics of the books I'd written (all unpublished and the source of a folder full of rejection letters from London publishers): one, the major characters were usually Scots; two, sense of place was to the fore; and three, there was a lot of violence. The solution suddenly came to me: write a crime novel set in Scotland, more specifically in my home city of Edinburgh.

Fair enough. This was before Ian Rankin had become a massive bestselling writer and well before the arrival of Alexander McCall Smith, so the competition wasn't as great as it would be now. But the distance I was from Scotland troubled me. Although I walked the streets of the capital every summer, I could hardly call myself a local any more. Solution – follow another of my favourite writers, George Orwell, and set the story a generation in the future. That way I could use the place more symbolically. The great perpendiculars of the Old Town suggest a potentially rapid descent from lofty intellectual achievement to the pits of sin, while the New Town's grey façades hide any amount of hypocrisy. I could also be satirical, as this Edinburgh was going to be an independent city state ruled by a supposedly benevolent dictatorship that followed the tenets of Plato (who was, of course, an admirer of the totalitarian city of Sparta).

That was the genesis of *Body Politic*, the first of what would be a quintet of novels featuring the maverick investigator Quint Dalrymple. Sense of place was essential to all of them. I sketched a map of Edinburgh and inked in the locations in a different colour for each novel. Eventually it looked like a toddler's scribble, so many were the marks. One of my main interests was in changing the use of buildings. The Castle became the headquarters of the Guard (the police force); the Assembly Hall was used as the temporary base of the Council of City Guardians (before they moved into the ransacked former Scottish Parliament). The city survived by running a year-round festival, with a tented casino in Charlotte Square and a racetrack in Princes Street Gardens. Holyroodhouse was destroyed in riots when the UK fell apart, while the Tollbooth Church was a strip-joint. It was an alternative vision of the capital, but reality sometimes came worryingly close. Not long after I'd closed off the tourist centre of the city to ordinary citizens, the Hogmanay Party organisers started doing exactly the same thing. Edinburgh folk seemed to take this fictional representation with restrained good humour, Glaswegians with louder guffaws. But expatriate locals were less impressed, 'How could you do that to our beautiful home town?'

I tried to explain that I'd been inspired precisely because Edinburgh is so rich in historical and architectural associations. And that it is a city so deeply lodged in the hearts of both residents and visitors that nothing a mere crime novelist could do would demean it. But eventually I began to feel bad about it too. Because I love Edinburgh. I love the sight of it, whether you arrive by plane, train or car – its vistas and parks, its spires and domes. I love the smell of the place, beer always brewing and the haar carrying in the salt tang of the Forth. I love the sound of wheels on the setts, the one o'clock gun that still makes me jump even though I try to pretend otherwise, the blast of fireworks during the Tattoo. I love the feel of the city – running my fingers along the chill damp of black railings, clasping a glass in a Rose Street bar, leaning against the warmth of red sandstone walls in the summer. Most of all, I love the taste of Edinburgh – 80 shilling ale, haggis and neeps, a Lowland malt splashed into life by a drop of water. The taste of home.

But sense of place doesn't stop there. Sense. Place. Imagination comes into play too, imagination aided by memory. I can sense places that I haven't been to for years. Kippford in Kirkcudbrightshire, where we spent rain-logged summer holidays; Rothesay, my mother's childhood home, touched only once through the hull of a Clyde steamer; the locks at Fort Augustus, where you either sail into, or escape, the abyss of Loch Ness; the vast red walls of Torridon, with Skye hovering in the sunset. These places are inside me still. Along with others I have never seen: George Mackay Brown's Orkney, an unfulfilled passion since boyhood, the skeletal remains of the German Fleet rusting away in Scapa Flow and the fishermen fighting the sea daily for lobsters; Sutherland, its great, desolate hills rolling away to Cape Wrath; the Western Isles. To my shame, I've spent years on a Greek island, but have never crossed to Skye's ramparts or tiny Raasay, to Lewis with its ancient stones pointing to early man's heaven, to Uist, Barra or Rum. Every name a poem, every village a repository of something more than history. And furthest off, St Kilda, now a parliament of ghosts, its hills standing up to the Atlantic storms, its sea birds no longer harvested. In my dreams I have been to them all. One day I will wake to a soundless smirr and look out across the Gaelic archipelago.

Of course, this isn't the whole story. Scots have always had a tendency to romance. We like to think we are fighters, survivors, and doubtless we have that in our DNA. The long generations of our ancestors who struggled with the land, its invaders, the climate and starvation – they must have left some mark. But we have also been losers, not just on the battlefield and in the stadium. We have been exploited by our own, ruled by kings and landowners who cared nothing for us and sent us to foreign lands rather than have the trouble of employing us. Later we were driven in our thousands to build the ships of empire and operate the mills that brought wealth to the few. So much for ancient fantasies of equality and fellowship. The rogue-sold Saltire is a tattered symbol. It is still worthy of respect, but with conditions attached.

A sense of place in contemporary Scotland should also include the needle-parks where young people waste away, the reeking pubs full of addled hard men, and the fast-food 'restaurants' where our children gorge themselves on poisoned pap. There is a new building at the foot of the Royal Mile that reflects much of our multifarious history in its structure. Can the Parliament become the centre of a new Scottish Enlightenment? Here's hoping, but don't hold your breath. We're the children of David Hume. We take scepticism in with our mothers' milk.

But this is meant to be a celebration, so let's concentrate on the upside. Think of Neil Armstrong, descended from a Border clan, stepping across the dusty surface of the Sea of Tranquillity – the first man on the moon, and he has at least a dram of Scottish blood in him. He is looking back at the earth, as far from home as any exile has ever been. As the planet spins slowly on its axis, he sees every land mass. If he thinks about it, all across every continent, even on Antarctica, there are Scots. From Dunedin to Saskatchewan, from Buenos Aires to Moscow, from Glasgow to Athens (the Edinburgh of the South), the Scottish Diaspora has put down roots. From a small, craggy land scarred by wind and wave we have spread across the globe.

'Our infinite Scotland,' said Hugh MacDiarmid. There was a man with a sense of place.

Standing Stones at Little Sparta

Sara Lodge

Most words in a garden hang in the air only for a minute and vanish with the visitors who voice them. But at Little Sparta, the garden crafted in Lanarkshire by poet and sculptor Ian Hamilton Finlay, words are part of the landscape. Engraved in stone and wood and metal, words in this garden mark patterns, debts, beliefs. Their downstrokes and curves draw subtle attention to those of the world they inhabit. Finlay revels in juxtapositions between man-made and naturally occurring art: the relationship between a fallen column and a tree, between a tortoise and a tank, an acorn and a hand grenade, between the crozier of a fern and a question mark. To wander in the groves of Little Sparta is to be invited into constant dialogues. Each fresh corner has its own riddle, dedication, quotation, anagram, epigram, or epitaph. Glimpsing Finlay's cut-outs of Apollo chasing Daphne through a copse, you too can hunt hidden treasure: a bird's nest sculpted into the fork of a tree, or a half-concealed stepping stone in a stream, engraved with the word 'Ripple'. But Little Sparta also has the solemn stillness of a garden of remembrance, its broken tablets commemorating the fall of civilisations and the fleeting tenancy of 'Man A Passerby', as one grave stone announces.

Like all magical gardens, Little Sparta is secret until you are inside it. There is no marker on the forgettable country road beyond the village of Dunsyre. Only the sight perhaps, of a few other cars on a verge in the middle of nowhere will alert you that you are in the right place. A steep, rough farm track, climbed on foot, brings you to a gate like a long, low wooden portcullis, which reads 'das gepflügte Land · the fluted land'. Looking back over it in autumn you can see the wordplay echoed in the ploughed (gepflügte) fields, which stretch away like fluted columns. In summer you can imagine Apollo playing his pipes among the flocks. The fields around Little Sparta are intrinsic to its classicism; it is a Vergilian enclave, an idyll, but one that constantly engages rather than denying the world around it.

I have two favourite places in this garden. One is its highest point, looking down toward Lochan Eck, where you can see the garden in its most expansive relationship with the hills, the farmland and moor beyond its bounds. The rich peat brown of the soil, the bruised purple and copper of heather and bracken are startlingly lovely. This is the palette and texture of the low-lands where I was born: wind-hewn rocks, undulating fields, clear blue harebells and rowan berries redder than a postbox. Here Finlay has built three dry-stane dykes, each with a gap in them just wide enough for two people to pass abreast. These punctuated walls read:

LITTLE FIELDS   LONG HORIZONS
LITTLE FIELDS LONG FOR HORIZONS
HORIZONS LONG   FOR LITTLE FIELDS

The relationship between the words beautifully captures the romance between contained space and uncontained space. The

lines of wall that frame the surrounding countryside are at one
with the broken lines of words, conveying our simultaneous
human desire for the finite and the infinite. Serious play is
everywhere here, from the notice among the trees that reads
'Bring Back the Birch' to the signpost for 'the Siegfried Line'
that points to Finlay's flapping washing.

The references to conflict and revolution are no mere ges-
tures. Little Sparta has been a battlefield. Since the 1970s,
Finlay has been defending it against incursions from Strathclyde Regional Council demanding money – and seizing
artworks in lieu of it – as a rate charge on a structure that
Finlay regards as a temple, a religious building. Finlay and his
supporters have been known to man the gates with pikes and
hoes. For Finlay, not only his temple, but his garden is an article of faith: the refusal of the council to credit it as such is just
further evidence of the modern world's scorn for piety. Finlay
is, at 80, a recognisably Scottish character: weathered, lean, an
artisan-intellectual, a boat-builder, land-lover, and question-
begger. Like Hugh MacDiarmid, Tom Leonard, Douglas
Dunn, Liz Lochhead and Carol Ann Duffy, he belongs in the
great tradition of Scottish bolshy *vis*: the force of opposing, of
the thrawn tree that grows against the wind and is shaped by
it into a whorl of wood that looks as if it is flying off the planet
at an angle. Poetry and Scotland have always been kin. Small
nations, small notions on the page, with an influence wholly
disproportionate to their size.

My other favourite place in Little Sparta is the grotto, which,
like the Roman pantheon, has an open circle at the apex of its
roof, which is overgrown with grass, bramble and honeysuckle.
Niches in the wall hold busts of Dido and Aeneas. Standing
here in the mossy dark, watching the clouds pass in that lens
of sky, I have often imagined the doomed lovers meeting here,

as they do in the stormy cave of Vergil's *Aeneid*. Ancient principles certainly do embrace in this cave, shrine, broch, with its delicate interior frieze and rough exterior, covered in living thatch.

Iain Hamilton Finlay has made, at Stonypath, a place that is all Scotland and yet points in every direction to the world beyond. Humorous signs across the garden walls really do direct you to Dieppe, as if it were the next village. Classical Rome, Revolutionary Paris, Wartime Berlin are only a few milestones away. Many modern gardens make statements: about their owners' taste, or means, their urbanity, or their internationalism. But statement gardens, like brash hosts, crave only admiration, not reply. By contrast, Little Sparta is a garden that delights in those tensions that stretch the mind to discover itself. A stile that leads across the garden's boundary bears the legend: gate – thesis; fence – antithesis; stile – synthesis. Many of the word ladders in Little Sparta illustrate such areas of transition: bridges, paths, stiles. They embody a garden's capacity to create distinct spaces that yet are formally and imaginatively connected to everything around them. No garden speaks more eloquently of our proper relationship to all that has preceded and all that will succeed us.